Robin Nolan's

BEGINNER**GYPSY**
JAZZGUITAR

Master The Essential Skills of Gypsy Jazz Guitar Rhythm & Soloing

ROBIN**NOLAN**

FUNDAMENTAL**CHANGES**

Robin Nolan's Beginner Gypsy Jazz Guitar

Master the Essential Skills of Gypsy Jazz Guitar Rhythm & Soloing

ISBN: 978-1-78933-198-1

Published by www.fundamental-changes.com

Copyright © 2020 Robin Nolan

Edited by Tim Pettingale

www.fundamental-changes.com

Over 11,000 fans on Facebook: **FundamentalChangesInGuitar**

Instagram: **FundamentalChanges**

For over 350 Free Guitar Lessons with Videos Check Out

www.fundamental-changes.com

Contents

A Message From Robin – Watch This First!

I'd like to cordially welcome you to the beginning of your Gypsy Jazz guitar journey. To make the most of our experience together, follow the link below or simply scan the QR code with your smartphone camera. I'll walk you through how to maximize your enjoyment of this book, and make the most progress in the shortest amount of time. See you there!

Short link:

https://l.robinnolan.com/hvugd

Introduction

My Gypsy Jazz journey began the night my dad and I drove from England to the Django Reinhardt Festival in Samois-sur-Seine, France. It was the start of an incredible adventure – one that has never stopped and has brought so much joy to my life.

Before the festival, I'd only heard scratchy recordings of Django, and they didn't inspire me in the same way as my other guitar heroes, like Angus Young or Eddie Van Halen. But arriving in Samois-sur-Seine, all that changed forever. Meeting Django's people, the Manouche, and hearing Sinti gypsies playing guitars outside their caravans, with campfires burning and wine flowing, was life changing. I'd never experienced anything like it. This was not like the scratchy recordings – the music was rocking, magical and full of romance. I knew immediately that this was the music for me. I wanted to learn to play guitar like that!

I'd taken my guitar with me and my dad pushed me to join in, but I was terrified. How could I keep up with these guys? They had such a loud, clear sound and I knew my Ovation acoustic was not going to cut it. Also, I didn't know any of the tunes!

I really didn't know where to start with this music, but start I did. Back in England, Tony Williams, a friend of my dad's, began to teach me some of Django's tunes – *Minor Swing, Douce Ambiance, Dark Eyes, Nuages*. I lapped up every note he showed me. Soon I formed a band with Tony called Trio De Samois and in due course we had enough material to make a recording. With our new album, the three of us piled over to Amsterdam and busked in Leidseplein (the main square). It was the start of a ten-year stint playing on the street. We never left and I still live in this amazing city.

Looking back, I can see that the key to us improving was repetition. Every day we played on the street, with the same set, sometimes for eight hours. I got comfortable soloing over the chord progressions and began to find my Gypsy Jazz voice. Fast forward to today and I'm sitting here writing this book, more than excited to help you start *your* Gypsy Jazz journey. Above all, I want to give you a taste for what this music is all about. Beyond the scales and exercises, I want you to experience the same magic and romance I experienced when I first encountered the music of Django and the gypsies.

I've always played this music in my own way and have been fortunate to build my life and career around this genre. I've found my own voice and this is what I want you to strive for too. Don't worry about trying to play exactly like Django, Stochelo Rosenberg or Biréli Lagrène – keep the elements of whatever style you play and mix it with Gypsy Jazz. Bring *yourself* to the music. Remember, Gypsy Jazz is not just a technique, it's a feeling, a way of life. Don't forget the romance!

About this book

In this book I want to give you the essential tools, techniques and inspiration to begin playing this music. Here are the core principles of my teaching approach. They are simple mantras that will help you to progress.

Keep It Simple. This applies to both rhythm and soloing. At every step, ask yourself, "Can I simplify this?" The answer is nearly always yes. Simplicity helps the music. Cut down on the thought process and use more heart and intuition.

Be Yourself. You will never play exactly like Django Reinhardt, but you are the best at playing like *you*. Always keep that in mind and don't feel any pressure to sound more "authentic". You'll stand out more this way.

Have Fun. Make sure you have fun at all times! You don't need to suffer in the practice room. In fact, you don't need a practice room at all! Get outdoors and play your guitar in the park, on a terrace, or at your local café.

Stay Inspired! This is my motto and something you should always seek. Listen to Django, watch the beautiful film *Django Legacy,* or do whatever inspires you. Watch how it magically improves your playing!

The material here is based on a teaching system I developed that has been used by hundreds of students all over the world. It has been carefully crafted to give you a solid foundation for a lifetime of enjoyment spent playing this wonderful music. There are five main areas to work through to become a great Gypsy Jazz guitarist. I call them the *Five Pillars of Gypsy Jazz.*

We'll address each pillar in turn. My aim is to help you learn the style quickly and simply, cutting through the confusion that many have about the "right" way to play it. Without getting bogged down in unnecessary theory, I'll show you the essentials, so that you can quickly start making music. Here's an overview of where we're going:

Pillar 1: Rhythm

In this chapter I show you the essential chord shapes used in Gypsy Jazz, then break down every single rhythm you'll encounter in this music. The Gypsy Jazz swing rhythm is the essence of this style and I can't stress enough how important it is to *get this* – it's part and parcel of the authentic sound of the music. I'll teach you how to make the music swing, how to use the upstroke, the Latin rhythms used in Gypsy Jazz and much more.

Pillar 2: Soloing

In this chapter I give you the tools you need to improvise over Gypsy Jazz tunes. I'll show you the simple system I use to create solos: a combination of tried and tested Gypsy Jazz licks, my own licks, appropriate scales and arpeggios, and the art of flow and trusting your ear. Here you will learn some very practical ways to spell out the chord changes and make your music engaging.

Pillar 3: Gig-ready Bootcamp

How to prepare for a jam session or gig is an important, but rarely taught aspect of playing – yet it's the glue that holds everything together. It's one thing to practice in the safety of your own home, but what about when you get on stage? Here we will address useful techniques such as how to start and finish a tune, and even how to combat nerves to free you to play the music you love.

Pillar 4: Playing Together and Making Music

Pillar 4 covers the art of playing with other musicians – another aspect that is often learnt the hard way! Here we will discuss jam session etiquette, how to count in a tune, when and for how long to take a solo, soloing in "fours" and "eights", and how to craft your own arrangement of a tune. This is vital information, whether you intend to play in a duo or with a full band.

Pillar 5: Capstone and Moving Forward

I call the final pillar the *capstone*. In this chapter I'll help you to consolidate everything you've learnt and help you move forward as a player by maximising your practice time. I will help you to focus on skills that will pay off at the jam session and consolidate techniques that will save you lots of learning time.

We will also discuss what it takes to stand out as a Gypsy Jazz player: how to carve out your own identity rather than going with the crowd.

Summary

I advise you to work through all five pillars systematically. Mastering rhythm comes before mastering soloing for a reason! All the great Gypsy soloists you have come across are also great rhythm players. The material here is designed to set you on the road to becoming a *complete*, competent Gypsy Jazz guitar player, rather than someone who just dabbles in the style.

Above all, I want you to relax and enjoy learning how to play this music. Gypsy Jazz is a joyful music and it's important to have fun playing it!

Robin.

Get the Audio

The audio files for this book are available to download for free from **www.fundamental-changes.com.** The link is in the top right-hand corner. Simply select this book title from the drop-down menu and follow the instructions to get the audio.

We recommend that you download the files directly to your computer, not to your tablet, and extract them there before adding them to your media library. You can then put them on your tablet, iPod or burn them to CD. On the download page there is a help PDF and we also provide technical support via the contact form.

For over 350 Free Guitar Lessons with Videos Check out:

www.fundamental-changes.com

Over 10,000 fans on Facebook: **FundamentalChangesInGuitar**

Instagram: **FundamentalChanges**

To learn more Gypsy Jazz guitar with Robin Nolan visit:

www.GypsyJazzClub.com

YouTube: **www.youtube.com/GypsyJazzSecrets**

Facebook: **www.facebook.com/GypsyJazzSecrets**

Instagram: **www.instagram.com/RobinNolan**

Bonus Online Resources

As a bonus this book comes with 22 videos, available to view online, that walk you through the various exercises. Perfect the techniques taught in this book by visiting:

https://www.fundamental-changes.com/robin-nolan-beginner-gyspy-jazz-guitar/

Short link:

https://geni.us/gypsyvideos

Or scan with your smartphone:

This book also comes with a Spotify playlist of Robin's must-hear tunes! You can explore it here:

https://geni.us/gypsyplaylist

Pillar 1: Introduction to Gypsy Rhythm Playing

In this chapter I want to teach you the essential Gypsy guitar chord shapes. There are, of course, many chord shapes you *can* play, but the majority of the Gypsy repertoire hinges on a small group of relatively simple shapes. In the second half of this chapter, we'll put some of these shapes to work as I show you all the rhythms you'll encounter in this music. Throughout, I'll make mention of relevant tunes from the Gypsy repertoire that you should check out.

Gypsy Jazz Chord Shapes

The purpose of the chord diagrams that follow is to equip you with practical shapes for Gypsy rhythm playing. Guitarists can get too hung up on exotic chord inversions – especially in jazz – but when it comes to playing this style of music, simple is usually better and the primary focus must always be on providing a solid rhythmic foundation.

Major Chords

First, here are three major chord shapes:

The first and most obvious is the straightforward major barre chord but notice that the high E and B strings are not played. For authentic Gypsy-style rhythm, it sounds best if only the bottom four strings are strummed to create a solid, powerful sound.

The chord is constructed from the notes G (root), D (5th), G (octave) and B (3rd). Check out the tune *Hungaria* by Django Reinhardt – the opening eight bars can be played with this chord as the progression moves from G major to G# major and back to G.

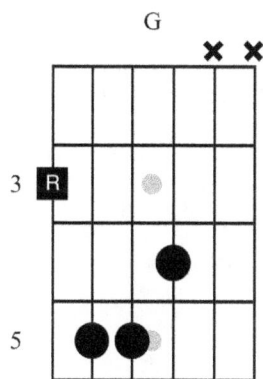

The next chord is the major 6th – illustrated here with a D6. In Gypsy Jazz, it's common to voice chords with the 5th as the lowest note. Normally, a D6 chord is constructed D (root), F# (3rd), A (5th) and B (6th). Here, we play it A (5th), D (root), F# (3rd) and B (6th).

Since Gypsy Jazz is played almost exclusively on acoustic guitar, this voicing enables us to strum the bottom four strings, and it avoids having to play too high up the neck. It still captures the sound of the D6 chord, and with the 5th in the bass, it will dovetail beautifully with the bass player who will be playing the root note.

You'll find it easier to mute the B and high E strings if you play the chord using all four fingers of your fretting hand, rather than making a barre with your index finger. The chord diagram below indicates the fingering you should use. This is the ideal chord shape to use on tunes such as *Daphne* and *Belleville*.

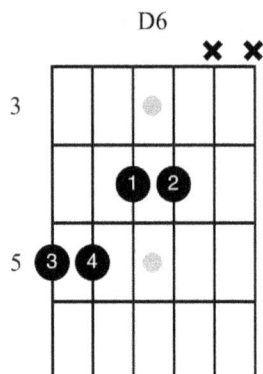

Here's a slightly more unusual voicing. If I'm playing in the key of C Major, I will sometimes use this shape to bring a different flavour. It's more of a stretch than the previous chords, but a useful shape to have in your arsenal for an authentic sound. The chord is constructed C (root), E (3rd) G (5th), C (octave) and E (10th).

Make sure you anchor your thumb on the back of the neck for this one – don't have your thumb over the top of the strings. Barre the 5th fret with your index finger and play the A string with your ring finger and low E string with your pinky. This is a great chord to use when you want to create a fuller sound. It's ideal for the introduction to the tune *J'attendrai*, for example.

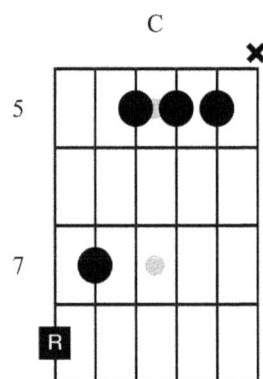

Minor Chords

Now we turn to three important minor chord voicings. They are all minor 6 chords. Rather than playing a straight minor chord or minor 7, the minor 6 brings out the unique Gypsy flavour.

The first is a simple but effective three-note voicing of Gm6. Normally, this chord would be constructed G (root), Bb (b3), D (5th), E (6th). The Gypsy Jazz way is to play the G (root), E (6th) and Bb (b3), with the other strings muted:

Gm6

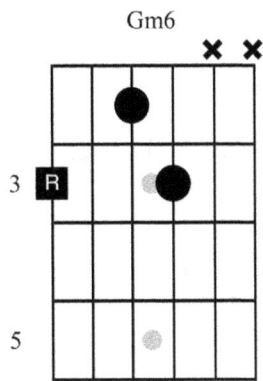

We can do a lot with this chord. For instance, we can play an entire minor blues using only this shape, without lifting the fretting hand off the strings.

Example 1a

Notice that in bars 9-10 we can still maintain the same shape to play the Eb7 and D7 chords. The same technique of moving the 5th to the bass note is being applied. These chords have no root note and are constructed:

Eb7 = Bb (5th), G (3rd), Db (b7)

D7 = A (5th), F# (3rd), C (b7)

When you listen to the audio example, you'll notice that it doesn't matter that there is no root in these chords – the context of the progression tells your ears what's happening.

The second minor 6 voicing has a root on the B string and looks like this:

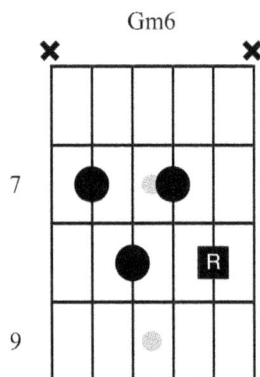

Gm6

If you're used to playing straight ahead jazz, you may instantly view this chord as an Em7b5 with its root on the A string. But Gm6 has the exact same notes and is constructed: E (6th), Bb (b3), D (5th), G (root). To quickly locate this chord, just think about targeting the root note on the B string, 8th fret.

Moving the 5th to the bottom enables us to play shapes lower down the neck for ease, and for a fuller sound. Try this Dm6 shape, played at the second fret:

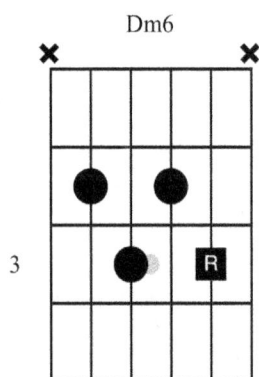

Dm6

This chord shape sounds great for a tune like *Dark Eyes*, where the first chords are A7 to Dm6.

The final minor 6 voicing introduces the thumb into the mix for the first time and looks like this:

Gm6

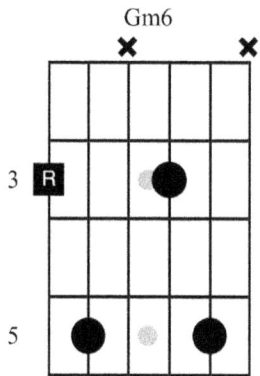

This chord is constructed G (root), D (5th), Bb (b3) and E (6th). From low notes to high, play this chord as follows:

- G bass note with the thumb

- D with the ring finger

- Bb with the index finger

- E with the pinky

The overall effect is more spacious sounding than the other voicings.

If it feels a little uncomfortable to use your thumb for the bass note, don't worry, this is normal! Persist with it and play the chord in different positions around the neck. Eventually it will begin to feel natural. We can see how useful this chord is when paired with a D7 chord in the chord progression below. It requires only minimal movement of the fretting hand to change chords.

Example 1b

Dominant 7 Chords

There are two must-know dominant type chords and the first one is another simple three-note voicing – in this instance A7 at the 5th fret. It is constructed A (root), G (b7), C# (3rd). Be careful to mute the other strings when playing it.

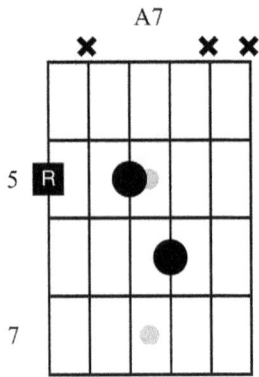

The second dominant 7 shape which is really useful is played like this:

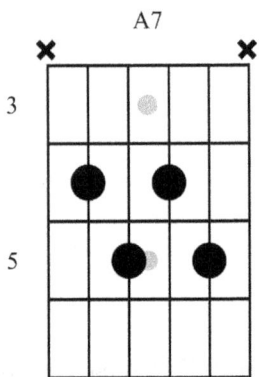

Notice that this is the same shape we used for the second of our minor 6 voicings. In this context, it can be seen as an A9 chord without the root, and is constructed: C# (3rd), G (b7), B (9th), E (5th). For an easy way to remember how to locate this chord, place your thumb over the neck and fret the A note on the low E string 5th fret for a moment. This will help you visualise where the root is. Again, you could use this shape for the beginning of *Dark Eyes*.

Diminished

Diminished chords are used frequently in Gypsy Jazz. Here are three shapes you need to know. The first is another three-note voicing and is played like this:

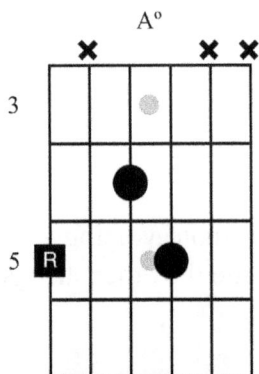

This is like an Adim7 chord with the b5 (Eb) omitted to create a smaller voicing. Here, the chord is constructed A (root), Gb (bb7), C (b3). If you encounter A° or A°7 written on a chord chart, you can play this chord.

Diminished chords are versatile because you can move them around the fretboard in minor thirds (three semitones from your original chord) and you'll still be playing the same chord, but with the notes in a different order. This is a sound you'll hear a lot in Gypsy Jazz. In the example below, the first Adim chord is played at the 5th fret. This is moved up a minor third to the 8th fret, another minor third to the 11th fret, and again to the 14th fret. In this example I've resolved it to a Gm chord.

Example 1c

The next useful diminished shape is a four-note chord arranged on the top four strings. It is constructed A (root), Eb (b5), Gb (bb7), C (b3). You can also move this chord around the neck in minor thirds and it will still be an Adim chord.

Try moving this shape while keeping an A bass note going.

Example 1d

There is one more common shape you will encounter, this time with its root on the A string. Here is a Ddim chord, constructed D (root), Ab (b5), B (bb7), F (3rd).

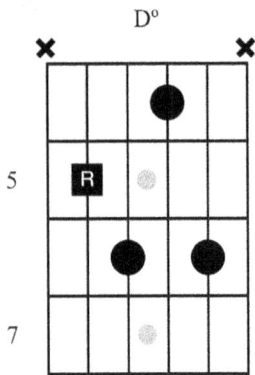

This shape is useful as a passing chord in a progression. In the key of C Major, for instance, we might have a turnaround of Cmaj7 – A7 – Dm7 – G7. We can use a passing C#dim chord in place of the A7 to create this movement:

Example 1e

The addition of the diminished chord creates a nice ascending chromatic bassline.

Augmented Chords

There are two augmented chord shapes that are frequently used in Gypsy Jazz. The first is an A7 augmented chord (often written on chord charts as A7#5 or A+). In the key of D Major, the A+ is the V chord, which strongly wants to resolve back to the I chord (D).

Here I'm playing the open A string (root), G (b7), C# (#5), F (3rd) and A (octave). You can omit the low A note and just play the smaller, four-note chord. It's easy to locate by its root on the high E string.

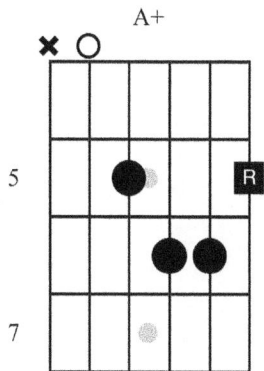

Another nice augmented chord uses this shape:

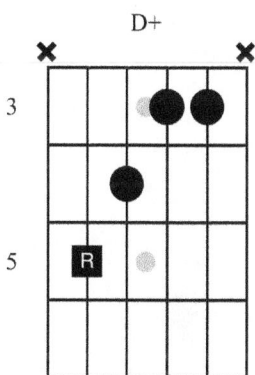

This time in the key of G Major, the V chord (D+) will want to resolve to the I chord (G). This chord is constructed D (root), F# (3rd), A# (#5), D (octave).

Dominant 7b5 and Minor 7b5

Lastly, I want to show you some useful "b5" chords. The first of these is the twin of the A+ chord – the dominant 7b5 chord. Based around a dominant 7 chord, it has a flattened 5th instead of sharpened 5th. In the key of D Major, the A7b5 chord wants to resolve to D. Here's the shape:

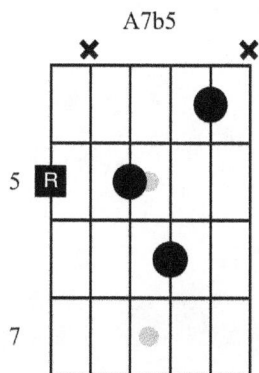

This chord is constructed A (root), G (b7), C# (3rd), Eb (b5). You'll notice is has a more dissonant sound than the augmented chord, and in isolation can sound a bit odd, but sounds great when resolved to a D6add9 chord:

Example 1f

You can also use an A7b5 chord to end a tune in the key of A Major, if you want it to feel unresolved and ambiguous.

Next we have two different shapes for the minor 7b5 chord. You will be familiar with one of these shapes – we've used it twice already!

The first has its root on the low E string and looks like this:

It is constructed A (root), G (b7), C (b3), Eb (b5). This chord usually appears as part of a minor ii V I progression. In the key of G minor, Am7b5 is the ii chord: Am7b5 – D9 – Gm.

Example 1g

The other important m7b5 shape has its root on the A string. Here is an Em7b5 in 7th position.

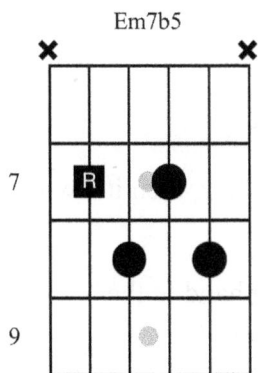

Paired with the A+ chord that we learnt earlier, we can use this shape to make a great sounding ii V I in D minor:

Example 1g1

We've now covered every important chord you should be familiar with. These will get you through 99% of the Gypsy Jazz repertoire. Now that you have a grounding in the essentials, we can move on to tackling the iconic Gypsy Jazz rhythm style.

Essential Gypsy Rhythms

The *keep it simple* mantra is the most important advice I can give to help your Gypsy Jazz rhythm playing. When you're out there playing, resist the urge to add unnecessary accents and fills. The best Gypsy Jazz player in the world is undoubtedly Biréli Lagrène, and the guy who plays rhythm for him is Hono Winterstein. What does he do? Very little! He keeps the rhythm very simple and leaves the fireworks to Biréli.

All soloists want is someone who can play in time. We don't want lots of chords, we want *groove*. Above all, don't slow down. This is the number one mistake rhythm players make. Practice maintaining the tempo and don't let it drag. Tap your foot and move your body. You are the engine of this music.

Rhythm is the vital element of Gypsy Jazz. This music has its own unique feel, swing and pulse. If you don't nail the rhythm correctly, it just doesn't sound like Gypsy Jazz. You're about to learn *La Pompe*, the chugging swing rhythm that is the engine room of this style. I've also broken down *every* common Gypsy Jazz rhythm you'll encounter. If you work methodically through this section, you will be prepared for virtually any tune that will come up in a jam session. Before we look at these rhythms, however, we need to fine tune the strumming and fretting hand techniques.

The Strumming Hand

The action of the strumming hand is very important in this style. If you're new to Gypsy Jazz, then it's worth taking the time to perfect this technique.

Unlike other styles of guitar playing, where you might anchor the wrist of your strumming hand to the body of the guitar, to achieve good Gypsy Jazz strumming technique you need to have a *floating wrist*.

When I strum a rhythm, no part of my hand, wrist or forearm makes contact with the guitar's body. I grew up playing lots of blues, so it took a while to train myself *not* to rest my wrist on the bridge. The floating wrist is needed to produce a strong attack, and therefore significant volume, because Gypsy Jazz guitarists usually play unamplified.

Tempos in this style of music can get very fast, so it's important to keep the hand/wrist fluid in order to achieve that speed. It's virtually impossible to play fast if your wrist is anchored or tense. Let's learn how to achieve the correct position.

1. Strumming arm position

First, rest the crook of your arm on the large upper curve of the guitar's body, as above. Your forearm should hang loose and be able to freely pivot up and down without touching the body. Try it now. Rest your arm on the upper bout and do an imaginary up and down strum. Keep your forearm and wrist loose and relaxed. The images below show the strumming position of the floating wrist/forearm.

2. The wrist

The wrist should remain loose and relaxed, so that it can freely pivot up and down. It may take a bit of training to get the wrist action right, but work at strumming up and down by pivoting the wrist. Be mindful of not resting it on the body or bridge of the guitar. Imagine you've lit a match and now you want to extinguish it by waving it rapidly up and down from the wrist – this is the action you are aiming for.

3. Holding the plectrum

The orthodox technique for gripping the pick is to press it against the side of your index finger at the first knuckle and hold it there with your thumb. The tip of the pick is pointing directly at the body of the guitar. Personally, I don't have an orthodox technique! I tend to "pinch" the pick between thumb and index finger. Arguably you might be able to produce more power and therefore more volume with the orthodox grip, but I suggest you use whichever way you find most comfortable, as long as you are able to maintain a floating wrist. I manage to make it work and so can you.

In terms of pick choice, I tend to use a Dunlop 2mm (the purple one). What you should look for in a plectrum for Gypsy Jazz is one that doesn't bend. This will give you the powerful tone and volume you need.

4. Strumming action

When strumming, the forearm will move a little, but most of the work is done by the loose, pivoting wrist. This is really important. If your forearm is swinging up and down in order to execute a strum, you'll never be able to play really fast rhythms. It all comes from the wrist action.

The Fretting Hand

The fretting hand doesn't often get a mention when teaching Gypsy Jazz guitar, but it's equally important to get right.

Like the strumming hand, the fretting hand also plays a role in producing the required tone and volume. In order to get the best tone/sustain, it's important to grip the neck quite tightly. A common feature of Gypsy Jazz technique is rapid vibrato on single notes, and to achieve this the fretting hand has to apply a strong grip.

To achieve this grip for single note playing, ensure that your thumb is locked against the back of the guitar neck, not curled over the top.

When it comes to rhythm playing, the fretting hand plays an important role in damping. The fast gripping/releasing action of the fretting hand is vital to achieve the most common rhythm in Gypsy Jazz. When playing rhythm parts, you *will* now bring the thumb into play (unlike classical guitar technique), as some chords require the thumb to play bass notes.

Pay attention to your technique as you now begin to play some rhythms.

Basic *La Pompe* Swing

La Pompe is the essence of Gypsy Jazz swing rhythm and essential to master as it forms the basis of hundreds of Gypsy Jazz tunes. If you nail this rhythm, you'll be prepared for the majority of the repertoire. *La Pompe* translates literally as "the pump" and is a very percussive rhythm style that essentially replaces the drums.

We've seen that many of the chords you'll encounter in Gypsy Jazz are simple three-note voicings, so to practice *La Pompe* we'll begin with an Am6 chord, consisting of the notes A, F# and C. Be careful to damp the strings that aren't to be played.

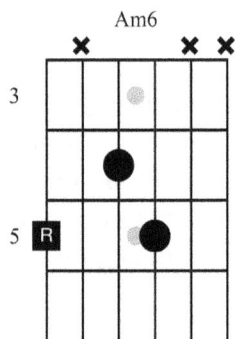

To begin with, we'll play the rhythm evenly in 1/4 notes – one downstroke per beat – giving each chord the same emphasis with a staccato attack. Let your strumming hand *fall* through the chord, pivoting as discussed earlier, to achieve maximum power. As soon as you've picked the G string (where the top note of the chord is located), lift your fretting hand slightly to damp the strings – you only need to strum the top four strings. The chord should sound clearly but cut off quickly.

Example 1h

Practice this example several times and get comfortable with the coordination between the fretting and strumming hands. The rhythm should be staccato, and no other strings should sound apart from the Am6 chord tones.

Playing this rhythm won't sound very exciting at first, but it's essential to master the mechanics of the strumming hand *attack* and the fretting hand *damping*, and really lock this into muscle memory. It's tempting to hit a bass note, then play the rest of the chord to create the familiar "boom chick" rhythm we've all heard, but don't! It's important to play it straight to begin with.

The next step is to apply a slight accent on beats 2 and 4. Listen to the audio download included with this book to hear exactly how it should sound. I'm playing beats 1 and 3 at a normal volume and hitting the strings slightly harder on beats 2 and 4. You should hear a subtle but discernible difference.

Example 1i

You are now playing the basic swing pattern. Each chord is still played for the same 1/4 note duration but beats 2 and 4 are prominent. It's not fancy – there are no ringing chords, no upstrokes, no double downstrokes – just a solid, driving rhythm that emphasises the backbeat.

Check out the playing of Hono Winterstein and you'll notice that the majority of the time he plays this very simple pattern. Listen to him laying down the rhythm on the up-tempo *New York City* on this book's Spotify playlist. This is what I'm talking about!

The most important thing you can do at this point in your playing is not to learn complex, impressive rhythms, but to develop really good time. Being able to play the simple *La Pompe* swing pattern with rock solid timing will set you up to be a great Gypsy Jazz player.

Set your metronome to a medium tempo and practice Example 1i over and over. Don't increase the tempo until you're playing perfectly in time, and then only little by little. Later, you'll discover that many tunes in the repertoire are played very quickly, so I can't stress enough how important it is to nail this rhythm cleanly and accurately.

One last piece of advice on playing *La Pompe*: many players think that they need to thrash their guitar to play this rhythm and play as loudly as possible. You don't! It can be played very subtly, especially if you are backing other instrumentalists – in fact, this will help it to swing more. Practice playing the rhythm with varied dynamics; the aim is to make the soloist sound good!

NB: As you get more into Gypsy Jazz, you'll discover that there are subtle nuances to *La Pompe* that suit certain songs and tempos. It's good to have some options, so if you'd like to learn more, I recently taught a live masterclass for my Gypsy Jazz Club, where I walked through every variation. You can see the Mastering La Pompe Swing Rhythm masterclass right here:

https://l.robinnolan.com/kzvqk

Upstroke Rosenberg Style

Don't be tempted to rush on from *La Pompe* until you've really nailed the rhythm – take your time and play it until it feels really natural. When you're ready, you can explore the many subtle variations to this foundational Gypsy rhythm.

The first of these is a rhythm that focuses on the *upstroke* accent and was made popular by the great Jimmy Rosenberg. When played up to tempo, the overall effect of this rhythm is more lilting than the basic *La Pompe*. Let's slow it down and analyse what's happening. There are fast upstrokes that occur before beat 3 and after beat 4 – just before the next beat 1. It's easier to hear this rhythm than read it, so first watch the short demonstration video at:

https://geni.us/gypsyvideos

Now let's break down the strokes that make up the pattern. In the space of one 4/4 bar, the rhythm begins on a downstroke and ends on an upstroke, so lends itself to being continuously looped. This is what the strumming hand is doing during one bar:

- Downstroke

- Downstroke

- Upstroke

- Downstroke

- Downstroke

- Upstroke

You can count the rhythm "1, 2, and 3, 4 and". Listen to the audio and try strumming the rhythm.

Example 1j

There is a lot of debate about where the upstroke should be placed in this rhythm in order to capture the right feel, and this can confuse players who are just getting into the style. I think of it like this: the upstroke should be crammed in at *the last possible moment* before the next beat of the bar!

Here is a good exercise to train yourself to hear the upstroke pulse: count out loud "1, 2, 3, 4 and, 1, 2 3, 4 and…" etc. (We're focusing on the second upstroke only). Leave each "and" until the last possible moment before the next beat falls.

Now try it with the full rhythm, placing two "and" counts into the bar:

"1, 2 *and* 3, 4 *and*, 1, 2, *and* 3, 4 *and*…".

Be sure to practice this with a metronome to really lock in the groove. Now play through Example 1j again. You'll need to spend plenty of time with this to lock in the pattern, so don't feel the need to rush ahead.

Watch the Upstroke Rosenberg Technique and Workout videos at:

https://geni.us/gypsyvideos

The Gypsy Bossa

Although many Gypsy Jazz standards are written with a swing rhythm, the Gypsy Bossa is an important rhythm to learn. There are lots of cool tunes that use this rhythm, such as *Bossa Dorado* and *For Sephora*. To learn the rhythm, we'll play it over chord changes similar to the first eight bars of *Bossa Dorado:*

| Dm | % | E7 | % | Em7b5 | A7 | Dm | A7 |

In Gypsy Jazz the bossa is a strumming rhythm and each bar is identical. Let's break it down and see what's happening. The strumming rhythm can be thought of as simply: Down-up-down-up. Its distinctive sound comes from the fact that the second downstroke is *muted* immediately after it's played:

Down-up-*down*-up

Execute the mute by lifting your fretting hand slightly or by palm-muting the strings with your strumming hand. It's important to keep the strumming hand moving steadily down and up, so use whichever method feels natural to you. The overall effect should be to provide a backbeat to your rhythm. Have a careful listen to the audio example first, then try it for yourself.

Watch the Gypsy Bossa Technique and Workout videos on the Fundamental Changes website.

Example 1k

Set your metronome to a comfortable tempo and increase the speed gradually. Your goal is to create that strong backbeat groove.

You'll always begin this rhythm with a downstroke, but once it's looping around, you'll find yourself changing chords on an upstroke. This is fine! To avoid any gaps in the strumming, you can move to the next chord in the progression fractionally before you strum it.

I recently created a video lesson for a student to help him break down the Gypsy Bossa and give it a solid, groovy feel. It's available for you to see here: **https://l.robinnolan.com/bu35z**

The Gypsy Bolero

Django Reinhardt wrote a few tunes that use the Gypsy bolero rhythm, such as the popular *Troublant Bolero*. As a rhythm guitar player, this is a useful rhythm to have under your belt, and it's often fun to adapt other tunes to this style (*Something Stupid* by Frank Sinatra works really well).

In the example below, I'm playing a Gypsy Jazz voicing of Emaj9 played in 7th position – the first chord of *Troublant Bolero*. As usual, the 5th of the chord (B) has been moved down an octave to the bass note, with the 3rd (G#), 7th (D#) and 9th (F#) stacked on top.

Emaj9

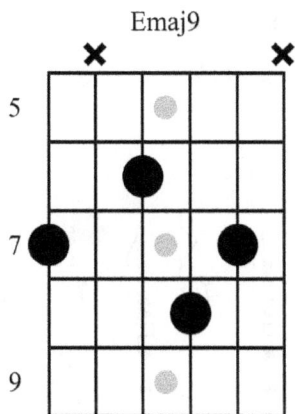

The strumming rhythm is a two-bar pattern and can be broken down as follows:

Bar 1:

- Downstroke

- Down-up-down-up

- Downstroke

Bar 2:

- Down

- Down

- Down

- Down

This can be played two different ways. In Example 11, the chords are allowed to ring freely (except for the rapid down-up-down-up movement):

Example 11

Alternatively, the pattern can be played tightly for dramatic effect, with all the accents staccato.

Example 1m

Practice the two examples above and aim for accuracy in your strumming and a consistent volume. The trickiest part to master is the rapid *down-up-down-up* movement. The strumming hand is doing most of the work here, so I recommend just strumming the muted strings while you are working on your accuracy.

Watch the Gypsy Bolero Technique and Workout videos on the Fundamental Changes website and be sure to check out The Rosenberg Trio playing *Troublant Bolero* on the Spotify playlist.

The Gypsy Samba

Of all the Gypsy rhythms, the Gypsy Samba is one of the most challenging to play, but that's what makes it one of the most exciting. When you nail this rhythm, it just sounds great. Check out the Rosenberg Trio's version of the Duke Ellington tune *Caravan*. They play it as a samba and Nous'che Rosenberg is a master of this rhythm.

We're playing this rhythm using a C7 chord with the 5th (G) in the bass.

This rhythm begins with a downstroke and only contains 1/16th note downstrokes and upstrokes. If it was played evenly, over the space of one bar you'd play a straight 1234, 1234, 1234, 1234 rhythm. What gives the rhythm its samba feel is the accented beats.

To begin with, just practice strumming a straight 1/16th note rhythm with your strumming hand to ensure that it's clean and consistent.

The notation below shows which beats are accented. In the first group of 1/16th notes, beats 1 and 4 are accented. In the second group, only beat 3 is accented. This pattern repeats in the second half of the bar. If you set your metronome to a 1/4 note pulse, and count just the accented notes out loud, you'll find yourself counting 1, 2, 3, 1, 2, 3 in the space of one bar. It's this "three over four" pulse that gives the samba its characteristic lilting feel.

Example 1n

Lightly hold down the C7 chord, so that the strings are muted. Only apply pressure with your fretting hand on the accented beats, so that they really pop out. Listen to the audio example to hear how it should sound. It's your fretting hand that is doing all the work to create the samba pulse.

Example 1o

A top tip for playing this rhythm at a faster tempo is to keep things light. Don't dig in and strum too hard. You don't have to apply lots of effort to make this groove. Keep your strumming hand very relaxed. When you're feeling brave with this rhythm, have a go at the opening bars of *Caravan*!

Example 1p

Don't forget to watch the Gypsy Samba Technique and Workout videos on the Fundamental Changes website.

The Gypsy Waltz

Played Gypsy-style, the waltz has a distinctive flavour and can be played by hitting bass notes followed by chords or just strummed. There aren't too many tunes in 3/4 time in the Gypsy repertoire, but one famous tune you should definitely check out is Django Reinhardt's *Montagne Sainte-Geneviève.*

We're going to play the waltz the first way, based around an open E minor chord. As we're in 3/4 time, the count is 123, 123 etc. In bar 1, hit the low E string, then play the rest of the chord twice, allowing the notes to ring out. In bar 2, play the A string second fret as the bass note, then play the chord. Alternate the bassline for each successive bar.

Example 1q

Example 1r incorporates this idea into a simple progression of Em7 to B7. Play the alternate bass note on the B7 chord by moving your middle finger over a string, while holding down the rest of the chord. The aim is to pick out the bass notes loud and clear.

Example 1r

When played the second way, we will typically be using a closed barre chord. We'll play an E minor barre chord in 7th position. The pattern is spread over two bars. In the first bar, each beat is played straight with a downward strum, but with an upstroke just preceding beat 1 of the second bar. Bar 2 contains three downstrokes, all on the beat. Count it like this: 1 2 3 and, 1 2 3 – with the upstroke on the "and". Watch the Technique and Workout videos on the Fundamental Changes website.

Example 1s

The Gypsy Finger Bossa

This rhythm is a Gypsy-style bossa but played with the fingers for a gentler feel. We'll play it using a standard Gmaj7 chord. The rhythm is executed with a downstroke on the bass note, played with the thumb, followed by an upstroke played with the fingers. This is followed by a staccato upstroke with the fingers.

Before playing the quick upstroke, I lightly "smack" my thumb onto the bass string, which serves the dual purpose of muting the string and making a percussive sound. It creates a nice backbeat for the rhythm. You'll hear me do this on the audio example. Have a listen then try it yourself.

I often play Django's *Nuages* using this rhythm, and it also sounds beautiful on *Tears*.

Example 1t

Playing Ballads Rhythm

I really love playing ballads and often include them in a live set. If I'm soloing, it's really important to me how the rhythm guitarist plays the ballad, and it can make a huge difference to the feel of the song, so I want to pass on some tips here.

The first thing to know is that playing a ballad is not like playing a swing rhythm only slower! This approach invariably sounds terrible. Instead we need to caress the chord and really bring the notes out. However, we can still play with a purposeful rhythm that keeps the tempo solid.

The next example appears to be very simple in its rhythm, with chords played four to the bar with a plectrum downstroke. But here's a tip for playing slow tempo tunes with good time: even though I'm only strumming 1/4 notes, I move my strumming hand *as though* I'm playing 1/8 notes.

Here is the notated example. The chords are the opening bars of *Nuages*. (NB: in the second half of bar 1, I'm playing an Eb9 with its 5th (Bb) in the bass).

Example 1u

Although only the 1/4 note strums are written, I'm playing a "ghost" downstroke between every beat, *without* touching the strings. You'll see a lot of Gypsy Jazz players do this. Why? Because when playing very slow, it's easy to think you're keeping good time when actually you're not! The strumming arm, however, is like the pendulum of a clock. Keeping a quicker, regular rhythm going makes it easier to hit the 1/4 note beat perfectly in time. Set your metronome to about 70bpm to practice this example.

It can be very effective when accompanying a soloist to play the chords as above while the melody is being played, but then play a staccato pattern at the beginning of, or during, their solo to add drama. Notice the downstrokes between beats.

Example 1v

Watch the Technique and Workout videos on the Fundamental Changes website.

You're now equipped to recognise and play all the Gypsy Jazz rhythms you'll encounter in the repertoire, and you've learnt the most common chord shapes. To complete this section, here are several exercises that will help you to develop and refine the different Gypsy rhythm skills. You can build exercises like these into your personal practice regime. Videos of each of the exercises are available on the Fundamental Changes website at: **https://geni.us/gypsyvideos**

Pillar 1 Rhythm Exercises

The first exercise is a *tremolando* strumming pattern that acts as a great way to loosen up the wrist of your strumming arm.

In Exercise 1 strum with muted strings. To a modest metronome tempo, first play 1/4 notes, then 1/8 notes and finally 1/16 notes.

Exercise 1

Exercise 2 is a Gypsy wrist-builder exercise, built around a basic *down-up-down-down* strumming pattern. The strumming pattern loops to make this continuous pattern:

Down-up

Down-down-up

Down-down-up

Down-down-up etc.

Again, play this with muted strings and focus purely on the strumming arm movement, with a good arm/wrist/hand position, as illustrated at the beginning of this Pillar.

Exercise 2

Exercise 3 is a workout designed to strengthen the fretting hand. We'll take a D6 chord and play *La Pompe* style swing with it. Practice the fretting hand *squeezing* action to fret, then quickly release the chord. The squeeze falls exactly on each beat and the quick release produces the staccato sound we want.

Exercise 3

Next, here is a swing-building exercise to help you refine your *La Pompe* feel. Play this with muted strings. It consists of short, staccato strumming hand downstrokes with an emphasis on beats 2 and 4. Set your metronome to 120bpm and loop this around until you feel that you have the swing feel really in the pocket.

Exercise 4

Now play the exercise again, but this time sounding an Am6 chord:

Exercise 5

Gypsy Rhythm Domination

As a bonus for this book, I wanted to give you access to an hour-long Gypsy rhythm video lesson, taught by my brother Kevin and me. It's taken from a training course we created called *Gypsy Rhythm Domination*. Kevin is one of the best Gypsy rhythm players around – I taught him! You can find it the video here:

https://l.robinnolan.com/63ytt

Pillar 2: Introduction to Gypsy Soloing

In this chapter we'll begin to look at the art of Gypsy Jazz guitar improvisation. This is a potentially huge topic, but as with Gypsy rhythm guitar, we'll move straight to the *essentials* that will have you playing authentic licks quickly, with a minimum of theory. Like learning any language, we'll start with some useful phrases that will begin building your Gypsy Jazz vocabulary. Making great music is our primary aim and I want to equip you with some great licks to set you on your way.

I've broken our study into three areas to get you soloing quickly:

Scales and arpeggios – Although you will probably know much of this information already, here we'll cover the basic scales and arpeggios that are important in Gypsy Jazz.

Licks – You'll learn some juicy licks you need to know for each chord type: major, minor, dominant 7, diminished and augmented.

Ear training – Lastly, I'll share with you a great ear training drill you can apply to any tune and show you how to spot the good notes (and the bad notes!)

If you work to combine these three elements, you'll be well on your way to being able to compose some awesome solos.

Scales and Arpeggios

The Major Scale

First and most obvious is the major scale. There are plenty of books that will show you how to play this scale in every possible position on the fretboard, but here I'm passing on the positions that I use all the time, which in Gypsy Jazz tend to be simpler. Here is the G Major scale played horizontally across the neck in 3rd position. You should be very familiar with this sound.

Exercise 1 – G Major scale

Now, here is the scale arranged vertically. When you ascend a scale across the range of the fretboard, there are a few options for *transition points.* In other words, the point at which you need to change strings to continue to play the notes of the scale. I've chosen transitions point that makes sense to me, but experiment and see what other ways you can find to navigate the scale.

Exercise 2 – G Major scale, vertical

Finally, here is the scale arranged vertically in the higher register.

Exercise 3 – G Major scale, higher register

The major scale is perhaps the most basic thing we learn as guitar players, but don't underestimate the value of knowing it thoroughly in all keys.

Firstly, the straight major scale is something you can fall back on if you get a bit lost in a tune, because it contains "safe" notes. When playing in the key of G, the G Major scale contains no "avoid notes".

Secondly, we can add chromatic notes to the basic major scale to spice it up and create simple but effective licks and phrases. Think of chromatic notes as "joining the dots" of the scale notes. To illustrate what I mean, here is a lick based around the horizontal G Major scale pattern in third position. Play it over a G6 or Gmaj7 chord.

Example 2a

Here's another idea that suggests a Gmaj7 chord shape and includes a chromatic run down on the high E string.

Example 2b

Finally, here's a major lick that takes a phrase and repeats it while ascending the scale and ends with a chromatic pattern.

Example 2b1

For homework, go and listen to some Gypsy Jazz standards written in major keys, such as *All of Me, Coquette* and *Swing 42,* and see if you can spot when the soloists add chromatic runs to their solos. Next, create yourself a medium-paced G Major chord vamp and experiment playing short phrases like the ones above.

Play some phrases using just G Major scale notes, then see what lines you can create by adding chromatic passing notes. Have a listen to the master himself, Django, playing some cool lines on *Swing 42* on the Spotify playlist.

Minor Scales

In musical harmony there are three common minor scales: Harmonic Minor, Natural Minor (also known as the Aeolian mode) and Melodic Minor (sometimes referred to as the Jazz Minor scale). This can be confusing for people who are just learning the guitar or wanting to get into jazzier styles of playing. I like to keep things simple and focus only on the Harmonic Minor scale. It is immediately evocative of the Gypsy Jazz sound, and I take the view that the subtleties the other minor scales bring can be added by the use of chromatic passing notes. Here are three must-know positions for the scale:

Exercise 4 – G Harmonic Minor arranged horizontally

Exercise 5 – G Harmonic Minor arranged vertically

Exercise 6 – G Harmonic Minor arranged vertically in the higher register

Take time to get really familiar with the sound and pattern of the scale. When you know the basic shape inside out, you can begin to add passing notes to create more interesting phrases. Try this descending line over a G minor chord.

Example 2c

Now here is a more complex line that really brings out the Gypsy flavour of the scale. Loop a G minor chord to jam along to and play this one slowly lots of times to let the sound of the scale sink in. Take your time with it!

Example 2d

Here is one final line that highlights the Gypsy flavour of this scale. Apply lots of fast vibrato to the Eb note on the G string, 8th fret.

Example 2d1

Now experiment over a G minor chord vamp. Play the scale lots of times to embed the sound in your head, then begin to add chromatic notes to create phrases. Listen to some classic Gypsy standards written in minor keys. There are plenty to choose from: *Minor Swing* and *Douce Ambiance* are great ones to begin with.

Major Arpeggios

As well as scale-based runs, you'll hear lots of arpeggio-based licks in Gypsy Jazz, so now we'll look at the essential major and minor arpeggios you should know.

Here is a major arpeggio shape I use often, in the two most common positions. Whole books have been written about arpeggios and a valid approach is to map the entire fretboard, so that you can play in every conceivable zone of the neck. Here, however, I'm concerned with giving you the most useful shapes for playing Gypsy Jazz, which tend to be arranged around the popular, simple chord voicings.

Here is a G major arpeggio arranged vertically, ascending and descending. This pattern covers a reasonably wide range of the fretboard. I use a quick slide on the G string, from fret 4 to 7, in order to shift my fretting hand position. The slide is reversed as you descend back down.

Example 2e

Here is the same arpeggio arranged an octave higher.

Example 2f

As with the major/minor scales, we can fill in the gaps in these patterns to create phrases and licks that have more tension and movement. Here's an idea that uses chromatic notes as a pedal tone (a repeating phrase that bounces off a common note):

Example 2g

Here's a more complex line which uses the same chromatic descending phrase an octave apart.

Example 2h

Minor Arpeggios

Here are the shapes I typically use for minor arpeggios. First, here is a horizontal arrangement of a G minor arpeggio in 3rd position, ascending and descending.

Example 2i

Now, here is the same arpeggio in the higher register.

Example 2j

We've established that what makes these arpeggios useful and interesting is the addition of passing notes. One common technique is to "anticipate" the arpeggio by playing an approach note a semitone below the root. Here's a simple line that uses this idea and ends on the 6th (E) of the chord. As straightforward as this idea is, it immediately creates the Gypsy Jazz flavour.

Example 2k

Whenever you find a nice line that you like, be sure to play it in other octaves on the guitar, as well as transposing it to other keys. Here's the same line played in the higher register.

Example 2l

Major Chord Licks

Unlike bebop or more modern styles of jazz guitar, Gypsy Jazz features less complex chord changes and has longer vamps on a single chord. This really lends itself to learning stock phrases which can be connected together to create longer lines. The more you add to your vocabulary, the more you'll begin to "hear" these lines for yourself. Here are three must-know Gypsy Jazz licks you can use over major chord types.

The first line is one I use a lot and is played over a G major chord. The line begins on the note B (the 3rd of the underlying G major chord) on the high E string then walks up chromatically to target a D note (the 5th of G major). The final three notes of the line spell out a G major triad.

I recommend that you play the first note of this lick with an *upstroke* rather than a downstroke, so that you hit the target D note with a strong downstroke.

Example 2m

Try applying this lick to some other chords. Remember that the lick begins on the 3rd of the chord, which you can quickly locate by ascending three steps up the major scale. (For instance, played over an E major chord, the line will begin on the note Ab).

Next, here is a great arpeggio-based line played over a C major chord, which illustrates how effective it can be to repeat phrases through an octave. The chord Cmaj7 is constructed C (root), E (3rd), G (5th) and B (maj7), and this phrase begins on the major 7th of the chord.

To play the first part of this phrase, use the index and middle fingers of your fretting hand in turn to play the notes on the low E string, and your index finger to play the E note on the A string. For the G note that follows, rather than using your pinky, shift your hand position and fret it using your middle finger. This will get your hand in the correct position to play the next part of the phrase. If you watch Gypsy Jazz players, you'll notice that they often play phrases that ascend/descend vertically across the fretboard, rather than horizontally. It's characteristic of this style of playing.

To end this phrase, you can execute the chromatic move from the note B to A on the B string with a slide and plenty of fast vibrato for authentic Gypsy Jazz flavour. This versatile lick sounds great whether played fast or slow. Try it in some different keys and at different tempi.

Example 2n

Our third lick is also played over a C major chord and has a slightly bluesy feel to it. It's the type of line that Django often played. You'll see right away that what makes this line so effective is the approach notes that target the strong chord tones, such as the Eb to E movement on the high E string, and the same movement repeated an octave lower on the G string. The approach note creates a moment of tension that is quickly resolved. This line will work great over a mid-tempo Django tune such as *Artillerie Lourde*.

With all these licks, make sure you can play them really cleanly. Play them well slowly before attempting them fast.

Example 2o

Minor Chord Licks

Now we turn our attention to three licks that work really well over minor chords. One simple thing you can always do is to adapt the vocabulary you already know. This first minor lick is similar to the one we played over G major, adapted to fit a G minor chord. Here is how it sounds:

Example 2p

Example 2o is a typical lick I might play over a minor chord. It captures the essence of the Hot Club/Django sound and is a great phrase that can be looped around. There are two things to notice about this lick. The first is its use of an "enclosure". In other words, we are *targeting* a note by playing approach notes that *enclose* it. The lick begins by targeting the note D on the B string, 3rd fret. This is the 5th of the G minor chord. It is enclosed by notes a semitone either side and played with a hammer-on/pull-off. Listen to the audio example and you'll quickly grasp how to execute it.

The second thing to notice is the rhythmic phrasing. Although the phrase is the same each time, rhythmically the strong notes fall on different beats in each bar. For example, in bar 1, the Bb note (the minor 3rd of the G minor chord) on the high E string, 6th fret, falls on beat 3. As the phrase loops around, the same note falls on beat 1 of the third bar.

This is just one way of playing this line. It's very adaptable, so put on your metronome and play around with it. Try beginning the phrase on beat 2 of bar 1 instead and keep looping it around.

Example 2q

Lick number three is an arpeggio idea that begins on the 9th (A) of the G minor chord. It's the same phrase repeated an octave apart. Play the first half of the phrase with all downstrokes and fret the adjacent notes at the 5th fret with your index finger, like a mini-barre. Slide up to the A note on the D string, 7th fret with your middle finger to reposition your hand for the second half of the phrase.

Example 2r

Dominant 7th Chord Licks

Jazz theory generally teaches students to use scales or modes that perfectly fit over dominant 7th chords (such as the Mixolydian mode). But while Gypsy Jazz has a lot of technical prowess and flash to it, it tends to be fairly simple in its theoretical approach. So, rather than learn a new set of dominant scales and arpeggios, I have a cool little hack you can use that works really well. When you see a dominant chord, you can play a minor scale or arpeggio whose root is a perfect fifth above it. For example, if the chord says C7, you can play G minor. If it's a G7, you can play something in D minor, and so on.

To locate the relevant minor scale, start on the root of the dominant chord and walk five steps up the major scale. If the chord is C7, play five notes of the C Major scale, starting on the low E string, 8th fret, and you'll arrive at the note G. I won't bog you down with the theory of why this works so well, except to say that superimposing the minor scale like this gives you all the great sounding notes that work over the chord, but you don't have to learn anything new.

Before you attempt the licks below, make yourself a slow-to-medium paced C7 backing track, and just play the G Harmonic Minor scale over it, ascending and descending. Listen to how the notes complement the chord and create a unique flavour. There is one tiny "clash" note – a C7 chord contains an E note, while G Harmonic Minor has an Eb, but this becomes a "tension" note that is quickly resolved and adds to the excitement.

Now, here are some licks using this technique. Listen to them carefully and get the sound in your head.

Example 2ra

Example 2rb

Example 2rc

Diminished Chord Licks

In Gypsy Jazz you will hear a lot of licks that have a diminished chord flavour to them. Here we'll learn two of the most popular. Django more or less invented this sound and you'll hear these ideas over and again in his playing. Diminished licks can obviously be played over diminished chords, but also create a wonderful sound over a dominant 7th chord.

The first lick uses the top three notes of a diminished 7th chord shape. The diminished 7th is a moveable or *symmetrical* shape. It can be moved around the fretboard in intervals of a minor 3rd (three semitones) and each time it is the exact same chord, just with the notes in a different order. In the notation below you'll see that the top note of the first chord is located on the 3rd fret. As the shape moves up, the top note is located on the 6th, 9th and 12th frets respectively (a shift of a minor third each time).

To play this lick, pick the top note of each chord shape with an upstroke, then play the remaining three notes with all downstrokes, using a controlled "push" through the strings. It will take a while to develop the pick control to make each note sound consistent and in time, so take it slowly to begin with and focus on picking accuracy. Let's hear how it sounds:

Example 2s

Notice that this lick is played over an A7 chord. In Gypsy Jazz, diminished licks can be used to spice up an otherwise bland sounding dominant chord. How can you easily transfer the idea to other dominant chords and why does this work so well?

Firstly, the correct diminished 7th chord will be located a semitone above the root of the dominant chord. For an A7 dominant chord, that's Bbdim7.

Why does it work? If we analyse the two chords, we see they have three out of four notes in common, and the diminished 7th chord has an added "tension" note. When superimposed over an A7 chord, the Bb note suggests a b9 sound.

A7	A (root)	C# (3rd)	E (5th)	G (m7)
Bb°7	Bb (root)	Db (m3)	E (b5)	G (6th)

You can use the lick over the first two bars of the standard *Dark Eyes*, which begins with an A7 vamp before resolving to Dm7. Once you have mastered the picking pattern and can play this lick cleanly, it can give the impression that you are playing really fast.

Sometimes in Gypsy Jazz you will encounter a diminished 7th or half-diminished passing chord, such as in the bridge of the tune *September Song*, which moves from C minor to C#dim and back to C minor. Here's a useful line that spells out the sound of the diminished chord. Play this line with down-up alternate picking.

Example 2t

Augmented Chord Licks

Lastly, here is a lick that can be used over an augmented 7 chord. It's less common to see augmented harmony in Gypsy Jazz, but it does crop up from time to time. For instance, you might see the movement Aaug7 to Dmaj7 on a chord chart. Sometimes this is written A7#5 to Dmaj7 or just A+ to Dmaj7, depending on the context, but A7#5 and Aaug7 share all the same notes.

The interesting thing about augmented chords is that you can move them up or down the fretboard two frets at a time as this lick demonstrates. It is played just like Example 2s.

Example 2u

Experiment with this sound, moving two frets at a time in either direction. You can just the chord, or arpeggiate it as in our example.

More on Chromatics

We've already seen that we can add chromatic or *passing* notes to major/minor scales and arpeggios. In fact, any lick, scale or arpeggio can be spiced up with the addition of chromatic notes, so think about adding approach notes or passing notes to licks you already know. You can even practice this technique by experimenting with the familiar pentatonic scale.

If we are playing over an A minor chord, we can play the straight A Minor Pentatonic scale:

Example 2v

Then we can add chromatic notes to connect the scale tones. Adding every possible chromatic note within the confines of this minor pentatonic shape gives us this pattern:

Example 2w

This, in itself, is not very musical, but we can pick out any chromatic notes we like to get creative and form musical phrases. Joe Pass once said, "You're only one fret away from a good note." Use your ears and experiment with chromatic notes until you discover a phrase you like. Here are a couple of ideas to start you off.

Example 2x

Here's an example of adding chromatic notes to the G Major scale, to create a lick over a G major chord vamp.

Example 2y

Ear Training Drill

Ear training is a frequently overlooked area of musical development but is a skill that can help you to identify chord changes and compose meaningful, musical-sounding solos. Once you have built a foundational knowledge of scales, arpeggios and licks, this exercise will help to unlock your creativity.

The exercise I want you to try is to play a constant stream of 1/4 notes. For the moment, forget about licks and rhythmic variations. Try this exercise over the chord changes to a medium-paced *Minor Swing*. Only play 1/4 notes – one note for each beat in the bar – but don't stop. Sounds easy, right?

It's interesting what happens when we impose any kind of restriction on our playing. This exercise is not as easy as you may think. There are no pauses in which you can think of a clichéd lick, so it forces you to think more melodically and to be creative.

If you do find it easy, then you should challenge yourself to navigate the guitar neck in different ways – use different registers, create lines that span the range of the neck etc. All this will deepen your understanding of the chord changes and what melodies can be played over them.

Here's an example that I improvised on the spot. Make a rhythm guitar backing track and experiment with it yourself. Keep going as long as you can and see what ideas emerge!

Example 2z

Here's another example, this time played a little faster.

Example 2za

This is a great way of mastering the harmony of a tune. If, at this point, you're a little uncomfortable about taking a solo on *Minor Swing* at a jam session, this exercise will help you to play through the changes and force you to use your ears to guide you, rather than mindlessly running up and down scales.

You can start very simply by playing basic arpeggios over each chord, then progress to scale tones, and eventually add chromatic passing notes. Work at this, and you'll find yourself playing much more musical etude-like solos that have a strong harmonic structure. If you feel like you are just playing licks over the changes all the time, this exercise will help you break through.

The Good Notes

I want to share some thoughts on the concept of the "good notes" when soloing. For me, understanding which are "the good notes" goes beyond simply knowing that a note happens to be a 6th, a 7th or a 9th – it means understanding the *character* of those notes and the emotions they evoke.

For example, over a Cmaj7 chord, playing a phrase that emphasises an E note (the 3rd of the chord), can evoke a happy, positive feeling.

A phrase that focuses on a B note (the major 7th of the chord) evokes a more romantic or melancholy feeling.

Example 2zb

A great exercise to do is to loop a chord – let's stay with Cmaj7 – and play random notes over it. Listen carefully and decide which are the "good notes" according to your taste. What feelings do they evoke?

Personally, I really like the sound of the 6th over a major chord. For Cmaj7 the 6th is an A. Play a Cmaj7 chord for yourself, then target the A note on the high E string, 5th fret, by walking up to it chromatically from the 3rd fret. For me, the 6th has an optimistic, bright, fresh quality to it. It's also very common in Gypsy Jazz melodies. Next, try the 9th (D) over the Cmaj7 chord. What does it say to you?

Now experiment with an A minor chord. What notes can you superimpose over the chord, and what feelings do they conjure? If you play an A minor barre chord in 5th position, what about an F# note on the B string, 7th fret? That's the minor 6th. What about the minor 9th (a B note on the high E, 7th fret)? What are the good notes in this context – the notes that make you feel something?

Continue to experiment, so that you begin to move beyond scales or arpeggios and really connect with the music.

A Simple Approach to Soloing

As guitarists, we are often prone to overcomplicate things when soloing. There is always the temptation to play something clever that will impress other musicians, but simple is better and nearly always more effective. When learning to solo over Gypsy Jazz standards, my advice is to start really simple. The more you listen to this music, the more you'll realise that soloists tend to strongly outline the chords, so begin by following the changes closely before attempting anything clever. Before we go further, here are my top tips to help you become a good soloist:

- Practice improvising over actual tunes. No one will ask you to play an arpeggio at a jam session

- Player slower with great tone and feel.

- Play within your technical capabilities and keep things melodic and grooving

- When you learn a new lick, integrate it into your playing immediately and apply it to tunes you know

- Adapt licks to make them your own – you don't have to play them the same as everyone else

- Don't be afraid to leave space. Good phrasing is more meaningful than a stream of notes

- Add vibrato, bends and character to your notes – don't hold back! Make your guitar sing!

Now let's get to some soloing ideas. We'll work on a minor blues. A good place to begin to compose a solo is to play a strong arpeggio, then shift it to accommodate the next chord in the progression. Here's an example in G minor. Although the idea is repetitive, it creates a strong melodic hook that your audience will relate to. After this first chorus, you can begin to vary and develop the main musical hook. Here I adjust the arpeggio slightly to fit the D7 chord.

Example 2zc

Check out the great Angelo Debarre playing Django's solo on the tune *Blues En Mineur* on the Spotify playlist.

The Bouncing Method

Next, I want to show you how to "bounce"! It's a term I came up with to describe how I solo over a set of changes. A solo can be simple in terms of its notes, but well-applied rhythmic ideas can really make it groove. Here, we are less interested in scales and arpeggios and more concerned with creating strong rhythmic motifs. Here's an example of what I mean, played over an A minor chord. The motif uses only two notes, yet makes a strong melodic statement.

Example 2zd

All this line involves is a simple movement between the 5th of the A minor chord (an E note on the G string, 9th fret) and the root note (A on the B string, 10th fret). It's all about the groove.

Once you've got this groove sounding "in the pocket", it can be extended across a whole progression by adjusting the notes to fit each chord. You might not always want to play an entire chorus using one idea like this, but here's how it sounds over the changes to *Minor Swing*. It's an effective way to spell out the chord changes. An idea like this will work beautifully at a higher tempo.

Example 2ze

Less is More

Fewer notes generally speak more than lots of notes in a solo. Space in a solo is a great tool and makes the notes you do play even more powerful. We can't all shred like Yngwie Malmsteen, so a less-is-more approach can really help us out! Gypsy Jazz can be challenging to play, but if you reach for those *good notes* and play them with a really good feel, you'll be connecting with your audience more strongly than if you are playing endless 1/16th note runs. Here's an example to illustrate how this works in practice.

The changes of the Gypsy standard *Daphne* feature a I vi ii V progression in D Major (D major – B minor – E minor – A7) and the tune is usually played up tempo. Rather than trying to match the tempo of the tune, you can play something like this.

Example 2zf

Instead of a flurry of notes, we have a strong melodic statement made with just a few notes. In bar 4, instead of playing the expected E minor to A7 movement, we have a dramatic Eb7#9 chord thrown in. This is a common b5 substitution. You can always replace a dominant 7 chord with another dominant 7 whose root is a flat fifth above. Just like the A7, this new chord strongly wants to resolve to the I chord of D major.

Another simple, less-is-more device is to play every note twice. This example takes the same melodic idea and adapts it, doubling up most of the notes. This line also makes great use of space. It's not necessary to fill the last bar here, so don't!

Example 2zg

Doubling up is another useful tool you can use when the tempo is haring along. Speed has its place, but you should always aim to first play beautifully those things that are well within your grasp, before resorting to more challenging ideas.

Even though we're only scratching the surface, I trust that the ideas in this chapter have given you some valuable tools to begin building your vocabulary. I'm learning all the time that when it comes to improvisation, repetition is so important – the more we play, the more the language evolves and expands. Here's a bonus video from my Gypsy Jazz Club – a masterclass called *A Simple Guide to Gypsy Jazz Soloing*.

https://l.robinnolan.com/4mbsm

Pillar 2 Soloing Exercises

To complete the second Pillar, here are some exercises to work into your practice sessions. They will help you to develop and refine the techniques we've discussed in this chapter. They also provide a creative way of learning to solo over chord changes.

How to Practice a Tune with Scales and Arpeggios

Whenever you learn a new Gypsy tune and want to solo over it, a good approach to mastering it is to first break down the chord progression and practice the scales and arpeggios related to the changes. In this example, I'll show you how I would approach improvising over the changes of *Minor Swing*.

As this is a *minor* blues, we'll use the Harmonic Minor scale. First, we'll look at the Harmonic Minor scale associated with each chord.

Over the Am6 chord = A Harmonic Minor scale

Exercise 7 – A Harmonic Minor Scale Ascending

Over the Dm6 chord = D Harmonic Minor scale

Exercise 8 – D Harmonic Minor Scale Ascending

For the E7 chord, rather than going into modal territory, Gypsy players will tend to use the A Harmonic Minor parent scale again, which achieves that classic Gypsy sound. It works perfectly well, as E7 is chord V of the harmonized A Harmonic Minor scale, so all the notes fit perfectly. Here is A Harmonic Minor, played descending this time, over an E7 chord.

Exercise 9 – A Harmonic Minor Scale Descending over E7

These three scales cover the main tonal centres of the minor blues. Now let's look at the arpeggios relating to each of the chords. Here are two positions for an Am6 arpeggio:

Exercise 10 – A Minor Arpeggio, 5th position

Exercise 11 – A Minor Arpeggio, 8th position

Here's a Dm6 arpeggio in 5th position.

Exercise 12 – D Minor Arpeggio, 5th position

For the E7 chord we have a choice. We can use notes from the A Harmonic Minor scale, but many Gypsy jazz players will simply play an E Major arpeggio over this chord.

Exercise 13 – E Major Arpeggio

In some versions of the *Minor Swing* changes two bars of a Bb Major chord precede the E7. This is a flat 5th substitution idea, typically found in jazz, where a chord is substituted with another chord whose root is a b5 interval away. Bb is a b5 above E7. The b5 sound creates a moment of tension that is quickly resolved when the chord changes to E7. I want to include this idea in the sample solo that follows, so here is the Bb Major arpeggio.

Exercise 14 – Bb Major Arpeggio

Armed with these tools, we can now practice soloing over the changes in a structured way. Get hold of a *Minor Swing* backing track (there are plenty on YouTube) and practice over the track like this:

- First, play the ascending/descending scale patterns for each chord over the backing track

- Next, play the ascending/descending arpeggios over each chord

- Now, blend the scale lines and arpeggios to begin to construct a simple solo over the changes

Don't worry if it sounds a bit robotic to begin with. This is an important exercise to embed the shape of the scales/arpeggios and hear how they work over the chords. To get you started, I improvised a couple of simple solos using these scales and arpeggios.

Exercise 15 – Solo 1

And here's one more chorus for you to learn.

Exercise 16 – Solo 2

Exercise 17 – Composing Solo Ideas Using Licks

Another method to get to know a tune and learn its harmony is to test out licks that you already know over the chord changes. Quite literally, if you know a nice minor-based lick in any key, transpose it to A minor and play it over the A minor section of *Minor Swing* to hear how it sounds. When the chord changes to Dm6, transpose the same lick to D minor. As you do this with different licks, you'll find that you begin to develop strong, melodic, motif-based ideas.

Here's an example solo to get your started, which uses some licks that I know. After playing through this, put on the backing track and try it yourself. Remember, *only* use licks for this exercise.

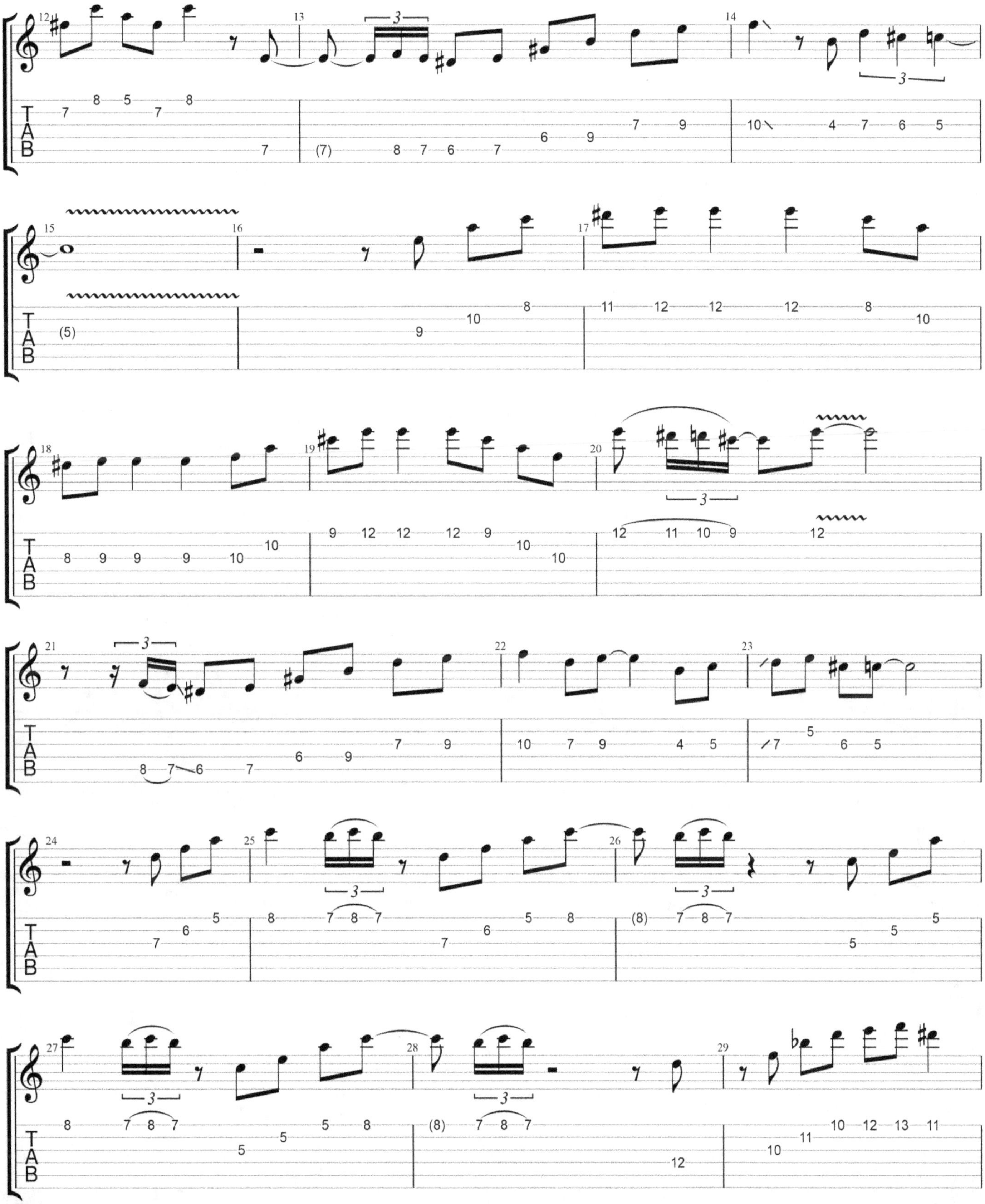

Exercise 18 – Practicing the "Bounce" Technique to Create a Solo

Earlier in this section we discussed the "bounce" technique – my name for developing a soloing idea from just a couple of notes. This is an idea worth pursuing, so below I've included an example for you to learn, after which you can develop your own ideas. In essence, I'm choosing just two notes per chord that spell out the changes. Rhythm plays a big part in this simple but effective technique, so you can be playful with it and don't be afraid to experiment!

Rather than transposing ideas around the fretboard, this technique is more effective if you stay in one zone of the neck and make small movements that define the chord changes. Here's how it sounds:

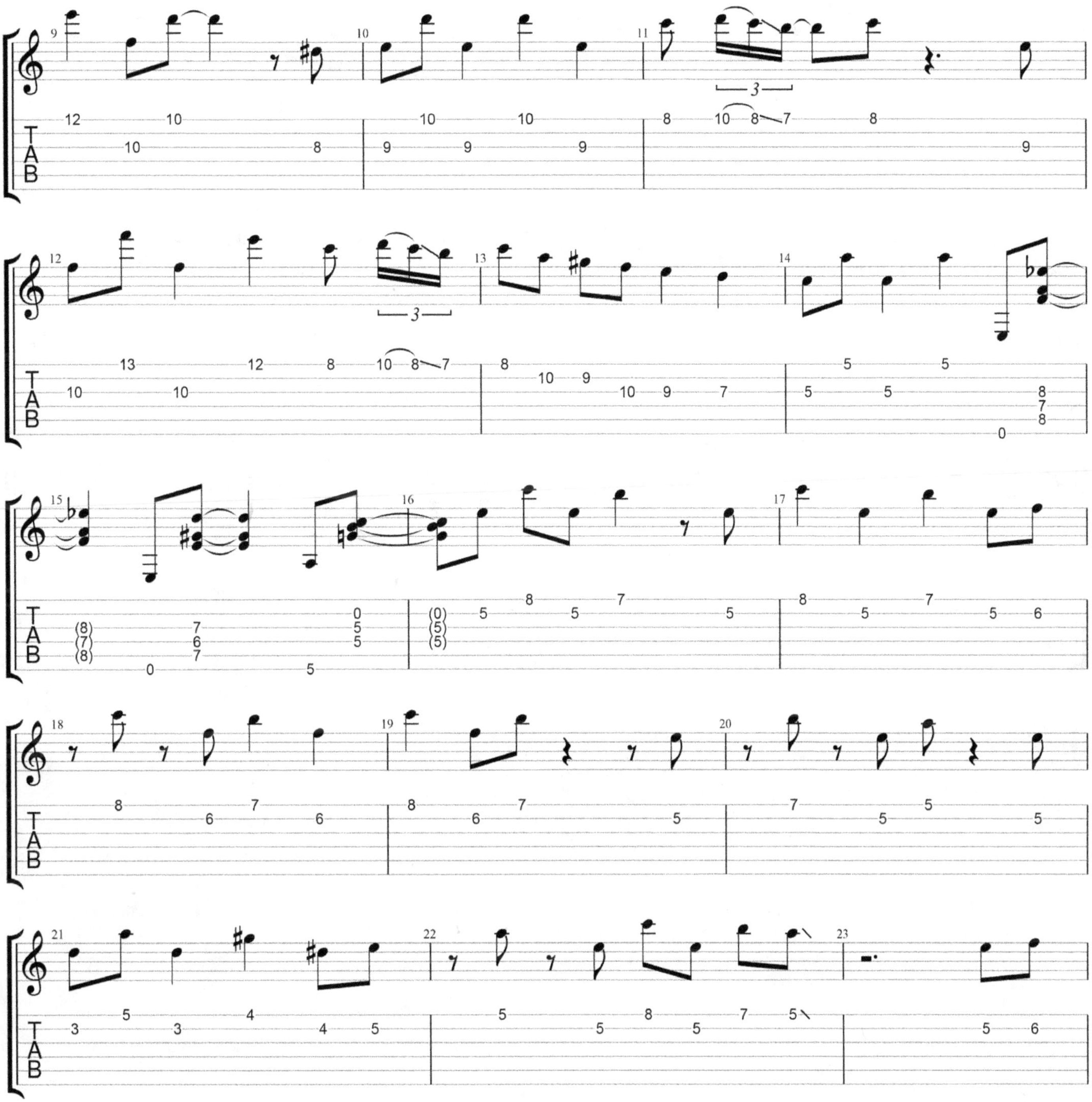

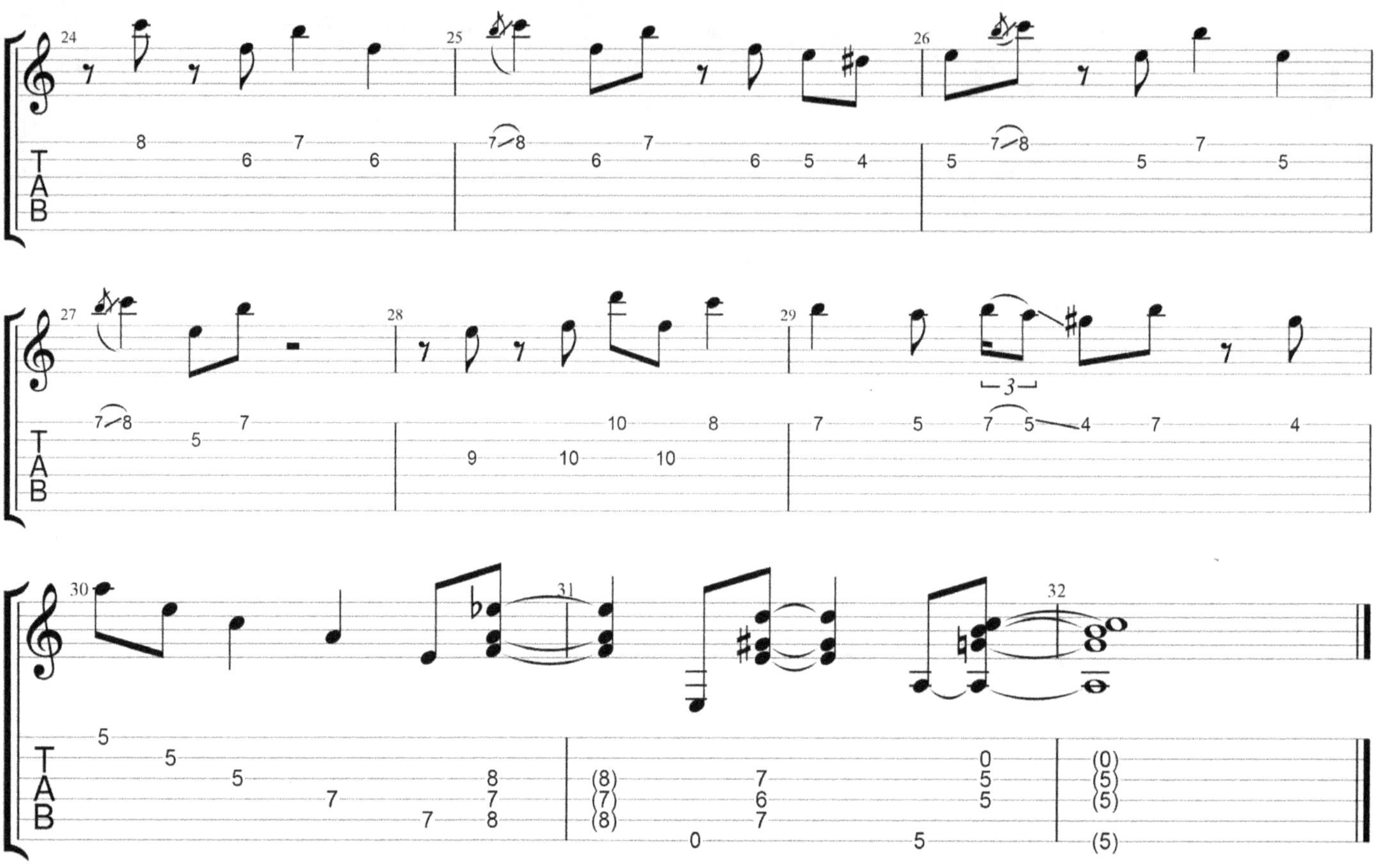

Pillar 3: Gig-Ready Bootcamp

Gig/Jam Session Survival Guide

There are lots of books and videos out there that teach chords, licks, scales, and how to solo over standard tunes etc., but virtually *nothing* that equips players with the tools they need for jam sessions or gigging with other musicians. I'm referring to:

- Solid ideas for beginning and ending tunes

- How to memorise tunes

- The essential tunes you must know

- How to conquer nerves and play with confidence

In this chapter I'm going to pass on some advice on each of these vital areas.

Intros and Endings

Let's get practical straight away and look at some options for starting and ending tunes. This is rarely taught, but it's so useful to have a few intro/ending ideas up your sleeve that are simple and dependable – and which make it clear and obvious to other band members what's happening. To begin with, let's look at a couple of intros that will suit tunes in major keys.

In keeping with our *keep it simple* mantra, these intros/endings set up the song for success without being overcomplicated or distracting. I've used them for twenty years and they just *work*. My advice to you is to get really good at playing a few choice beginnings and endings, rather than being mediocre at many. However, you can adapt them to your own style – you don't have to play them exactly as written. Vary them and make them your own.

Example 3a is a great intro for a tune in the key of C Major. I first heard Biréli Lagrène play this when he was a kid and its charm lies in its simplicity. The first chord is an inversion of C major – i.e. it has a note from the chord other than the root as its bass note – in this case an E note (the 3rd of the chord). It is often written as C/E.

This chord starts a chromatic bass note descent that is heading for the I chord of the key, C Major. C/E is followed by a three-note Eb diminished chord, which leads to Dm7. The last chord of the sequence is a G7 chord, but with the 5th (D) in the bass, so that the bass note remains constant. The G7 wants to resolve to the I chord of C Major, so the tune is nicely setup to begin.

This is the perfect intro for a tune like *All of Me*.

Example 3a

You should always transpose ideas so that you will instantly recall the pattern when faced with a tune in a different key. Here is the same intro transposed to G Major.

Example 3b

Here's another major key introduction that takes the previous idea and flips it around. Django starts the tune *Hungaria* like this and it's a well-known and loved intro. This time we begin on the I chord of the key and ascend, before descending back down to the dominant 7 chord that will resolve to the I chord. It's common to use diminished shapes as passing chords which connect chords from the key. This example is in G Major. A G# diminished chord connects the G major and A minor chords. Then a Bb diminished chord connects the A minor to the G major chord inversion (G with a B in the bass). The Bb diminished is played again as the progression descends, but this time we end on a D7 with an A in the bass to set up the tune. Once again, this idea is all about the chromatic bassline.

Example 3c

Here is the same idea transposed to the key of C Major.

Example 3d

You can just strum these intros, but they do sound especially good if you pick out the chromatic bassline as it gravitates to the I chord of the tune.

Next, let's look at a couple of reliable intros for songs in minor keys. The first example is in G minor and the main interest comes from the bassline. Even if you only play the bassline to this example, it still works. Ensure you make the bass part nice and punchy before introducing the chords.

The Gm6 chord is followed by a G minor inversion with the 3rd (Bb) in the bass. Then we have a minor ii V I sequence: Am7b5 – D7/A – Gm6.

Example 3e

Here's the same idea in C minor.

Example 3f

I'd use this type of intro to begin a minor blues or most minor tunes. An alternative to this is the *Hit the Road Jack* style approach. This sound will be very familiar to you as it has been used a lot – but it's used frequently because it's a strong intro and it's obvious where it's heading. Here it is in D minor.

Example 3g

This intro works well when played by alternating the bass note with the chord in the classic *boom chick* style. The sequence begins with the I chord of the key, D minor, and thereafter we are targeting the V chord, A7, that will resolve to the I chord. The method of getting there is adding other dominant chords to gravitate towards it (C7 then Bb7).

Let's hear how this sounds transposed to A minor. For this example, I've added an extra element at the end to lead back to the A minor. The progression rolls around three times, but the final time I'm targeting the E7 chord that will turn it around to A minor. First, we play a semitone above the E7 (F7), then a semitone below (Eb7) before hitting the E7. Listen to the audio to hear how it sounds and aim to play it confidently.

Example 3h

Now let's look at a couple of good ways to end a tune. It's important to be purposeful about how to end, otherwise it's easy to resort to the same predictable clichés. First, here is a melodic line you can use to end a tune in a major key. This will work well on a tune like *Lady Be Good*. The ending line is a melodic tag that replaces the last two bars of the form.

Practice this idea over the last four bars of *Lady Be Good*. In bars 1 and 2, strum the Am7 and D7 chords four to the bar. The ending line begins on beat 2 of bar 3 and we drop on a big G major chord to end.

Example 3i

Again, let's transpose this idea to the key of C Major. Here's just the ending line:

Example 3j

Here's a cool ending you might use on a minor blues. Like the previous idea, it spans the last four bars and uses a melodic line to signal the end of the tune. This example is in G minor.

Example 3k

Here it is again, transposed to C minor.

Example 3l

Creating a Killer Set List

One aspect of gigging that is often overlooked is the art of creating a good set list. When I'm backstage with my bandmates, scribbling down tunes, we are always anxious to pick the right tunes and place them in the right order to deliver the best possible show. In my experience of touring the globe, there are two basic scenarios to consider:

First, I'll often be gigging with a pick-up rhythm section I've met just hours before a show. You'll probably also be playing with different musicians at each gig or jam session. Again, keep things simple. Musicians often want to play complicated tunes/arrangements, but don't worry about playing *Minor Swing* or *All of Me* at every gig. Audiences love these tunes and they always go down well. Stéphane Grappelli played many of the same classic tunes for his entire career, and just got better at them!

Second, if you're gigging with your own band, then your set list can be more varied and include tunes/ arrangements that only you know. I wrote a tune called *Ravi* (for Ravi Shankar) that has some intricate patterns in it. But it would take up too much valuable rehearsal time to teach this tune to people who've never heard it. So, if you want to include some original or more obscure tunes in your set, make sure to surround them with well-known tunes.

Working backwards, you want to place one of your strongest songs at the end. For me, that might be something like *Joseph Joseph*. We have a big arrangement of that tune which includes a really fast, double-time section and it ends with a bang. Going out on a high is important!

Starting strong is equally important. You want to grab people's attention, so selecting a tune that is moody and ambiguous is often not the right choice. Instead, it's good to start with something reasonably up tempo that is bright and positive. *All of Me* or a nice major tune such as *Lulu Swing* is a good place to start.

As you progress through the set, think about how each tune will complement the previous one. Don't, for instance, put two major key swing tunes back to back. *All of Me* and *Swing 42* are both played in the key of C Major and have a similar tempo, so putting them together is not a good choice. Try alternating between major and minor keys, and if you *have* to place two major or minor tunes back to back, make sure they are in different keys.

Think about the contrast between the moods of the tunes as well. After an up-tempo major key tune, you can change the mood by playing a minor key ballad, or a moody bossa. After bringing the mood down, you might want to follow it with something exciting to lift people's emotions again.

With my trio we tend to have four big Latin tunes in our set. *For Sephora* and *Bossa Dorado* are the best-loved Gypsy bossa tunes. *Bossa Dorado*, written by Dorado Schmitt, is possibly the most popular non-swing Gypsy tune ever, and it's a killer that audiences love to hear.

We split up the Latin tunes by placing two in the first set and two in the second. It's a matter of distributing the songs, so that there is interest and variety across the entire set. Think about where the songs will have the most impact (i.e. a slow ballad played after a very fast tune will have more impact than following a medium-paced swing).

Conquering Nerves and Stage Fright

There are very few, if any, musicians who have not suffered everything from mild nerves to stage fright at some point. One night stands out for me. In 2009 I was invited by Bill Wyman of the Rolling Stones to play alongside my jazz guitar hero Martin Taylor at the Royal Albert Hall in London. It was a charity night with a special reunion of the Small Faces with Ronnie Wood, so there was an all-star line-up and the gig soon sold out. If that wasn't nerve wracking enough, my pregnant wife, Judy, had gone into labour in Amsterdam earlier that day and there was no time to fly back – the show had to go on!

As I arrived at the venue my phone buzzed. It was Judy's friend telling me I had a son! I didn't know what to do and passed the phone to Bill Wyman, who I'd just met backstage. He spoke to Judy and congratulated her, then gave the phone back to me and said, "You're on in twenty minutes!" Panic set in as I knew I was about to play the biggest gig of my life. *Okay, breathe Robin,* I told myself. And that's what I did – I found a bathroom and closed my eyes for a few minutes to compose myself.

Minutes later I walked out onto the stage with Martin Taylor and he told the audience, "I think Robin has something to tell you." I leaned over to the mic and proclaimed, "I've got a baby boy!" The applause was deafening and then we began to play *And I Love Her*, dedicated to Judy. It's a night I'll never forget.

Here are a few thoughts on how to conquer your nerves and give your best performance every time you step on stage.

Getting anxious before you play is a predicament for all creative people. One technique I use to counteract this is to find a quiet place and take a few minutes to have a mini meditation. It's good to still the mind, breathe deeply and be conscious of the present moment. Literally remove yourself from the pre-gig hustle and bustle and centre yourself before stepping back into it. This is a strategy that works for me.

If you're on stage and still feeling anxious, know this: *the anxiety will go away*. Often, we are our most anxious just before and at the beginning of a performance, when we're worried about everything. By the end of the gig, 99% of the time everything has gone great and we wonder what we were so worried about! Armed with that prior knowledge, you can relax and focus on enjoying the music in the moment.

You can also think about nerves differently. A rush of nervous energy produces adrenalin, and we can use this to our advantage. It helps us perform to the best of our ability, so it can be a good thing when it comes to music. Without it, we might be lazier about our playing or less focused.

It's also good to remember that your bandmates and the audience have not come out to see you fail; they all want you to do well! That night at the Albert Hall, the outpouring of love from the audience and musicians was overwhelming. It's all about making music together and enjoying it. Everyone wants the best out of the experience.

Of course, it's important to have done your preparation. Get your act together and make sure you *know* the songs! But once that's done, breathe, slow yourself down, know that the nerves will pass, embrace the adrenalin, and understand that everyone wants you to do your best. Stay cool!

Mindset and Focus

It's easy to lose focus when playing, so it's good to be mindful of this tendency we all have and be aware of directing our concentration.

If you are playing rhythm guitar, you should focus intently on the *time* and push aside all other distractions. One of the best ways I've found to do this is to give all my attention to the soloist. Adjust your position so that you are facing them, and serve them with the best supportive rhythm you've got. Too many times I see rhythm players daydreaming while someone is taking a solo! This is catastrophic for the music.

Often, Gypsy Jazz trios will consist of two guitars and an upright bass. Without a drummer, the rhythm guitarist and bassist are the primary timekeepers. Regardless of what anyone else is doing, your time should be rock solid and grooving. Be fully present in the moment and don't take your eye off the ball!

For soloists, it's equally important to live in the moment and fully invest yourself in the music. If you're thinking about what you're going to have to eat later, you're not in the moment! Your focus should be on the changes that are being played, so that no matter what you're doing, you're always totally aware of where you are in the song.

This kind of focus should spill over into our practice times too. It's very easy to be distracted or to practice in an un-focused, aimless way. Instead, we need to be purposeful about our practice times, with clear goals that we want to achieve and a clear path to get there. 10 minutes of quality time with a metronome is better than an hour of aimless noodling.

Back in 2000, my brother Kevin came to Amsterdam to join my trio. He couldn't really play guitar – he was starting from scratch. But he played the bass and I knew he had good time, so I was confident he could do it. The only way he was going to get good enough to perform with us, however, was to practice – and I mean *really practice*. He moved into the shed at the bottom of my garden and (appropriately) began wood shedding! One tune at a time he played the repertoire over and over. One day, the genius Gypsy player Jimmy Rosenberg came over and he and Kevin jammed. I remember thinking, *Wow! We have one of the best Gypsy Jazz guitarists in the world playing with a complete novice here, but they are sounding great!*

Kevin's goal was to play with a metronome and memorise ten tunes – enough for a gig – concentrating on time and rhythm, which he did for hours every day. When it comes to mindset and focus, remember this:

1. You can't deliver a solid performance if you're trying to remember the chords. Kevin and I sound convincing when we perform on stage because we've played the tunes thousands of times.

2. Good time is key. Treat the timekeeping with the respect it deserves. Practice with your metronome up loud, so there's no escape. Immerse yourself in the beat until you're locked in.

Memorising Tunes

Memorising tunes is something I'm really passionate about. I don't like seeing guys on stage with music stands and charts/iPads, and I don't think audiences want to see a bunch of musicians staring at charts, because then it's no longer a performance. It feels like the musicians haven't done their preparation and don't know the music, inside out. Although some people are very fluent sight readers, for many, creative energy will be wasted processing the information on the music stand – and that takes away from the performance.

My advice is to *really know* a good selection of tunes, rather than half-knowing hundreds with the assistance of a real book. It's one thing to flick through charts at a jam session, but that's not for the stage. Know the progressions to the tunes like the back of your hand, so that you can play them automatically without thinking. This not only helps with rhythm playing, but also soloing. Your solos will suck if you're thinking, *what's the next chord?*

What's the best way to memorise tunes? Some are easy because they are based on a predictable pattern, such as a minor blues. Others are more challenging. A tune like *Nuages* has a long form and lots of complex chords, which can make it intimidating at first. My advice is to break the tune down, section by section. Memorise one section at a time and play it over and over again. Know each section thoroughly before bringing them all together. Take just four bars at a time if you need to, and gradually add another four bars and another four bars until you have the whole tune. Get obsessive with the tunes you learn and play them every day. Think about the chords as you walk down the street and hum the melody. You must absorb them to play them with conviction. Remember, learn fewer tunes, but *own them*.

Another tip for memorising tunes is to look out for the changes that crop up regularly, such as the I vi ii V pattern that makes up the majority of *Swing 42*. This pattern is the same as the beginning and end sections of

I Got Rhythm, for instance. If you think about the patterns of chord progressions, you'll begin to spot them in lots of tunes, and this helps with remembering them.

The 5 Gypsy Jazz Tunes You *Must* Know

There are hundreds of standard tunes that make up the Gypsy Jazz repertoire, but there is always the core of tunes that everyone plays. If I was forced to distil this down to just five must-know tunes, then they are:

- Minor Swing

- Djangology

- Dark Eyes

- Sweet Georgia Brown

- Nuages

Get to know these tunes inside out and you'll be able to sit in on any Gypsy Jazz jam session, join in and have fun playing.

Minor Swing is so popular that it's invariably the first tune anyone new to the genre will learn. It's catchy, riffy and fun. It's the *Stairway to Heaven* of Gypsy Jazz! Whether it's a local jam session or a Biréli Lagrène gig – *Minor Swing* will be played, so own this tune!

Djangology is a fun, charming tune that really captures the spirit of the music and was written by Django himself. It's a big jam session favourite. The chords are pretty easy to learn, but it's harder to solo over than it appears, so it's worth spending some time working on it.

Dark Eyes is also really important to know. People have called it the "Gypsy anthem". It only has four chords, and the melody is really simple, but it's often played very fast which makes it challenging to solo over. In France it's known as *Les Yeux Noir* and in Germany, *Schwarze Augen*. It's a big audience favourite and you can guarantee they will clap along.

Sweet Georgia Brown is a tune I used to play with my dad in the pub in my teenage years. He would bang out the chords and I would play the melody and a solo. It's so famous that the audience always murmur their appreciation as soon as it kicks off. It's also a good tune for getting your soloing chops over dominant 7th chords up to scratch. Gypsy players will often play it at breakneck speed, but don't worry, it also swings nicely at a medium-up tempo.

Nuages is undoubtedly Django's most famous ballad. It has a beautiful, haunting melody that never ceases to move the listener. It's an incredible composition, so just learning the chords will improve your musicality and playing skills. It has everything: interesting, dynamic harmonic movement and a melody from heaven. It also sounds great as a solo piece which falls nicely under the fingers.

Pillar 4: Playing Together and Making Music

You've reached the fourth pillar and we're going to explore in more depth the art of playing with other musicians. Understanding how to work with other musicians is the glue that holds everything together, whether you're in a jam session, on a gig, or at a recording session.

The Art of Dynamics

One skill that sets apart great players from good players is the use of dynamics. Skilled musicians don't just focus on *what* they are playing, but *how* they are playing it. Light and shade is very important to the storytelling aspect of music, and this is what we should be aiming for: to communicate feelings and emotions to our listeners. We want to take people on a journey with the music.

In my own playing, I will use dynamics much more than impressive technique. One practical way of achieving this is to ensure that we don't play everything at one volume, whether that's quiet or loud. You might, for instance, play the rhythm part for *Minor Swing* at a normal volume while the melody is being played, but when the first person begins to solo, really bring down the volume and keep it soft and light. Bringing the volume down like this is really effective. Firstly, it brings the soloist into focus, and secondly, it means you've got somewhere to go with the music. After playing very softly, playing loudly is a big contrast. Soft to loud is so much more effective that loud to louder!

You can apply dynamics to every part of your playing, whether it's accompaniment, playing melodies or soloing. When there is good band communication and everyone is listening to each other, you can begin to play softer in your solo and the whole band will come down with you. I've been to gigs where the guitar player has played quieter and quieter, and witnessed the whole room come down with him. It's probably more attention grabbing than playing very loudly.

Creating Arrangements

My trio has played *Sweet Georgia Brown* for years, so we have a cool, polished arrangement for it. We start off half time, with a slow, raunchy first chorus, played by the guitars only. Then we stop and relaunch it, full throttle. The bass joins in and we speed into the solo, before screeching to a halt and resuming the half time feel. For good measure, we speed up at the very end for comic effect. A solid arrangement helps to make a tune a success. You can check out our version on the Spotify playlist.

In Gypsy Jazz (and more broadly across Jazz as a genre) the tunes tend to follow a similar form: the introduction is followed by stating the melody; the musicians improvise over the chord changes; the melody is stated again; then there is a planned or spontaneous ending.

With this predictable format, it's good to think of ways to spice up the arrangement to create more interest. Simple things can be highly effective – such as a dead stop and a bar or two of space in which the soloist begins, before the rest of the band join in. It creates a moment of drama. Another simple idea is to modulate up a key for the solos, which will give the music a real lift.

To stamp your identity on a tune, start by conceiving a really good intro. We've already looked at a couple of standard intros, but you can get creative and write your own. If you are playing a tune in D Major, for instance, you might set the tune up like this…

This is a pedal tone idea. Play a regular Dmaj7 chord in 5th position, then shift the upper part of the chord up a semitone but leave the bass note in place. Keep the D bass going throughout.

Example 4a

Having come up with an idea like this for the intro, it can be used again as an arrangement device to set up each new soloist.

One device that can work well is to play an introduction *rubato* (out of tempo), with rich chords interspersed with melodic phrases. Here's a tip to achieve this. Pick a chord progression you know well and work through it, alternating between chords and melodic figures. In *Minor Swing*, for instance, play the first A minor chord, then a short melodic phrase in A minor. Then move to the D minor chord and do the same. Continue through the full sequence. Even though it's partly improvised, it will have a strong structure and works well to set up a ballad.

Consider how the song will end. Could this idea be used again? To bring more variety, you might instead write a lick that the whole band will play in unison, which would be a powerful way to end.

Always check out other people's versions of the standards. There is loads of research you can do by listening to different approaches on YouTube. Or, if you are learning a specific song, search for it on Spotify and listen to the different versions that come up. This is a great way to discover arrangement ideas you can "borrow".

Working With a Bass Player

As a guitar player, you need to work harmoniously with each bass player you encounter. I've worked with many bass players and each had their own particular traits. Some bassists I've worked with played with a two-beat feel – kind of like the tuba in Dixieland music – which was rock solid timewise, but limited the band's ability to swing. I had the great pleasure of having Simon Planting in my trio for a few years, who combined two-beat with walking four to the bar. Currently, the bass player in my regular trio is Arnoud Van Den Berg, whose time and swing feel is the best I've played with.

At a jam session, it's critical to lock in with the bass player. Make eye contact – they will appreciate you paying attention to what they're doing. If it's your band, don't be afraid to tell the bassist what you need them to do. A good Hot Club style bassist will play short punchy notes – different to the Ray Brown style of modern jazz. Listen to some Gypsy bass players and pay attention to what they are doing. How does it affect the swing feel?

I get a lot of questions from students about how best to work with a bass player. "If I'm playing this chord, will it conflict with what the bass player is doing?" etc.

Communication is key. The rhythm section must work as a unit, so be open and discuss what chords you are going to play. Be super-clear about it. In many tunes, even ones as straightforward as *Minor Swing*, there are alternate changes. One version of *Minor Swing* borrows the changes of *Autumn Leaves*, for instance. If you're going to do something like that, the bass player definitely needs to know – don't leave it to chance! Agree at what point in the tune you're going to bring in this idea (for example, only during the solos).

Another tip when working with a bass player is to go easy on the bass notes on the guitar. If you're just playing with another guitarist, then it's appropriate to play those *boom chick* rhythms that drive the tune along. But a bass player will provide that bottom end groove, so the guitar player needs to play a part that is complementary. Straight-ahead strumming will work best. It will also work better to play small, three-note chord voicings than full chords. Less is more.

If the bass player is playing with a two feel, then you might play something very simple – 1/4 note strums. If he's playing a walking bass pattern, then there is more scope to vary what you play. You don't even need to play constantly – you can punctuate the rhythm with accents.

Playing Jazz 4's and 8's

4's and 8's is a technique used by all jazz musicians to create interest in a tune. After everyone in the band has taken a solo over the whole form of the song, they will take a short 4-bar solo, then the next person will take 4 bars, then the next, and so on. It's a great way of taking the music somewhere different, because much of the excitement in jazz comes from the interplay between the musicians. 4's is a great way to have a musical conversation with your bandmates, which is why it's often called "trading 4's". It's like the question and answer format of the blues.

This might cycle around a few times before the band play the melody again and end the tune. You'll often hear this technique used to give the drummer a solo. Sometimes the 4-bars is extended to 8-bars, depending on the form of the tune. It's definitely a technique you can use in jam sessions, but you can also build it into your arrangements to keep things fun and exciting. My only advice is" *don't forget to count!* It's so easy to lose your place in a tune, so make sure you keep counting and know where you are in the form at all times.

Turnarounds

Another great arrangement device is the turnaround. Sometimes a turnaround is built into the final bars of a tune, but if not, you can add your own. The point of a turnaround is to clearly signal that you've reached the end of the song and are about to begin again from the top. You want to create the feeling that the chord progression needs to resolve, so a turnaround will nearly always involve the V chord – the dominant 7 that strongly wants to resolve to the I chord of the key. In the key of C Major, the V chord is G7, so a good turnaround progression would be...

Example 4b

Another approach is to start with a C major inversion and descend to the G7 (a little like the introduction we looked at earlier).

Example 4c

You can also use the minor key introduction you learnt earlier as a turnaround at the end of a minor key tune. This one works great to replace the last two bars of a minor blues.

Example 4d

Accompanying With Walking Basslines

If you are just playing with another guitarist, then at times you may want to play a strong bassline as an accompaniment. For example, you might spell out the changes to *Minor Swing* with a bassline, punctuated with chords, rather than just strumming four to the bar.

Here's an example of something I might play over the first eight bars of *Minor Swing*. Work through this idea slowly to begin with, before playing it up to tempo. It's important to play it cleanly, so that the bass notes ring out and sustain, but the chords have a punch to them.

Example 4e

Where have all these extra chord changes come from, you may wonder! The idea here is to use notes from the parent scale of the key – in this case the A minor scale (A, B, C, D, E, F, G, A) – as bass notes, then build chords on top of them. To avoid playing the same note on two successive beats, you can add a chromatic passing note to lead to the next scale tone (like the C# that occurs in bar 2).

The chords are drawn from the key of A minor (Am, Bm7b5, C, Dm, Em, F and G), but you'll notice that I take a few liberties with them. It's a common feature of jazz to take a chord from the key but change its *quality* (changing a minor chord into a dominant 7 is particularly popular). Hence, in bar 6, the E minor chord becomes E7.

In the first two bars, the starting chord is A minor and the target chord is D minor. I'm adding B minor, C major and C# diminished chords to "connect" those two chords. In bars 5 and 6, the target is an E7 chord, so I target that chord with a chromatic descending idea.

You don't have to play a continuous walking bass line throughout the entire form of the song. This is the kind of idea you can intersperse to create interest. You can play four to the bar to begin with, then bring out the bassline to connect to the next section of the tune:

Example 4f

Here's one final idea to give you food for thought. If you come across a couple of bars containing one static chord, you can always use inversions of that chord to provide different bass notes and create a bassline. Let's take E7 as an example.

You could just strum it, like this…

Example 4g

Or you could play…

Example 4h

Instead of strumming two bars of the same chord, we're using inversions to create movement and momentum. An E7 chord is constructed: E (root), G# (3rd), B (5th) and D (b7). We use each of those notes as the bass note to create this nice line that uses the range of the fretboard.

To work on this idea on your own, it helps to know which chords belong to each key, so you may need to do a bit of theory homework. But experiment and see what different basslines you can add to the changes of your favourite tunes. Be guided by your ears – you'll instinctively know whether something sounds right.

Pillar 5: Capstone and Moving Forward

In the last of our five pillars we'll look at how to move forward with all you've learnt so far. In this section I want to pass on some tips and advice to help you hone your skills and maximise the time you invest into your music. The mantra of *have fun* is key here. I want to inspire you to go to a jam session, start a band, or even record an album.

Warm-up Exercises

Before the serious playing begins, it's important to warm up. There are certain things that I always do before playing to get relaxed and set myself up to play well. One useful exercise is the *tremolando* exercise (see the exercises section at the end of Pillar 1 to refresh your memory). Not only is this a great exercise to loosen up your wrist, but the technique has its place in Gypsy Jazz playing. Here are some tips on this technique:

1. Tap your foot, feel the pulse and keep time

2. Moving your strumming hand (with a floating wrist) as fast as possible

3. Don't grip the pick too tight

4. Don't dig into the strings too much, keep things as light as a feather

5. Practice over chord changes

Listen to the tune *Heavy Artillery* (or *Artillerie Lourde*) by Django on the Spotify playlist and you'll hear him strumming the chords to the bridge *tremolando*. It's quite a difficult technique to master, so it serves both as a warm-up and a technique builder.

Pick a tune, like *Minor Swing*, and practice *tremolando* on the whole progression. Work at getting the rapid strumming consistent and even throughout the progression.

For the next warm-up, pick a medium tempo tune, such as *Lulu Swing*, and just strum through the changes. Don't worry too much about dynamics and timing at the moment, you're just warming up. Play loudly and confidently. It's like you are waking up the instrument as well as yourself, so don't be shy.

Next, play some melodic lines. You can practice some arpeggios that span the range of the fretboard, or your favourite licks. There's no magic formula to this, you can play anything really. The point is to "wake up" your fretting and picking hand coordination and get things flowing as they should. Once you're warmed up, it's time for a focused practice session.

How and What to Practice

You need to practice, of course, but *what* you practice is very important to keep you moving forward. When I have one-on-one private Zoom calls online with my new Gypsy Jazz Club members, we make a plan that starts with a big goal, which I then break down into baby steps. We pick a few tunes that we want to get good at and apply all the techniques and skills to actual music.

It doesn't matter how much time you have to practice each day – whether it's half an hour or the whole day – *how* and *what* you practice is far more important. One tip I'd like to pass on is to divide up the time you have, so that you're not practicing just one thing and neglecting other areas of your playing.

To practice efficiently, only practice things you'll actually play on a gig. Relaxing and noodling on guitar is not practice, so keep the two activities separate. Here's a good practice regime for you:

1. Play some rhythm every day, if only for ten minutes. It will help keep your strumming hand loose and in the groove.

2. Make sure you've truly committed to memory the tunes you "know"!

3. Play along to backing tracks.

4. Hone your technique. There is no magic formula: play, play, play those arpeggios and licks until they sound clean and fluent.

5. Expand your repertoire by working on new tunes. Learn the melody and the chords before jazzing them up, and listen to as many different versions as possible.

6. Have fun and stay inspired!

The Metronome is Your Best Friend

We like to think our timing is pretty good, but the metronome doesn't lie! The metronome is your friend, because time invested here will feed every other area of your playing, as your innate sense of time is sharpened. Playing with a metronome will help you when soloing as well as strumming chords. My grandmother used to have an old-fashioned manual metronome which sat on top of her piano, and that's what I used when I was learning, but there are loads of customisable metronome apps available free to download to your smartphone, so there's no excuse not to have one!

When playing rhythm, make sure the metronome is nice and loud, so you can hear it clearly. Try practicing with four clicks to the bar to begin with, at around 80 beats per minute (bpm), and strum through a tune. When you're comfortably in time, try playing with the metronome keeping half time. In other words, set the metronome to 40bpm and focus until you can hear it clicking on beats 2 and 4. Now play the tune again, with the metronome keeping the backbeat. This can be hard to get right at first, but if you persist with it, you'll build a much stronger sense of time.

Leave the metronome on while you are practicing licks too. This helps keep the energy going and ensures that you don't become lazy (or rushed) with your phrasing.

Rhythm Practice

Put the metronome on and practice some Gypsy rhythm. Work on memorising a new tune. Remember, we don't want to be reading charts on stage if we can avoid it, so break the tune down into sections as discussed earlier, and practice playing the changes to your metronome. Begin with an easily manageable tempo and make sure you are really nailing the changes before you think about going faster. If you play fast before you've really locked in the rhythm, you'll just be playing badly faster! Interestingly, often where people lose time is when playing ballads more than very fast tunes. It takes more focus and a greater sense of time to play accurately at a very slow tempo, so it's worth practising ballads with a metronome too.

If you are practising a fast tune, start with a simple rhythm. Play all downstrokes – the most basic form of *La Pompe*. Get the rhythm really swinging before you do anything more complicated. When the downstrokes are sounding great, try introducing some upstrokes, Rosenberg style. Remember to keep your arm relaxed and your wrist fluid.

Learning New Tunes

If you have more practice time available, then learn the melody to a new tune. I cover the Gypsy Jazz repertoire in my Songbook System series. In these books I've written the melodies as simply as possible, leaving lots of room to add embellishment later.

https://l.robinnolan.com/m3nh2

It's really important to know the *actual* melody of a tune, and not someone else's way of playing it. Know the tune first and stamp your identity on it later. When you know the melody thoroughly, play through the tune lots of times and add simple embellishments to vary it. Gradually decorate the melody, step by step, and eventually you'll be playing a very musical-sounding solo that is rooted in the original tune. This will sound way better than noodling up and down scales.

Often, the process of learning a new song is thrust upon us. A few years ago, my good friend Dhjani Harrison invited me to play at his wedding and requested *The Rain Song*. I pretended I knew it, but after hanging up the phone I thought, *The Rain Song, what's that?* Having googled it, I discovered the epic Led Zeppelin masterpiece and got to work figuring it out! It was tricky, but I managed to craft a cool instrumental arrangement for the trio which sounded awesome on his big day.

Learn New Chords

This might sound simplistic, but I have a technique for memorising and practicing new chords that always works:

1. Fret the chord and make sure it sounds clean when you strum it.

2. Remove your hand from the guitar for a few seconds.

3. Bring your hand back and re-fret the chord.

4. Repeat, until your hand perfectly remembers the shape and goes back to the chord every time without a problem.

It's worth taking this time to be laser focused with your chord playing. Work on one chord at a time and take it slow.

Stay Focused

It's important to practice things you are actually going to play at a gig/jam session i.e., actual tunes! Getting more confident with the repertoire and how to play it is what will move you on as a musician. If you practice soloing over *Minor Swing* every day for a week, next week you'll notice a tangible improvement in your playing. It's better to practice real music than theoretical concepts; all our theory of scales and arpeggios is just a means to an end.

Jam Session Etiquette

Over the years I've participated in hundreds of jam sessions. All the major Django festivals have them and I've found myself playing *Minor Swing* with the best players in the world. I've been sandwiched between Stochelo and Jimmy Rosenberg so close that I could feel the hot air coming off their picks as they played one fast chromatic run after another! What I've learnt is, don't try to play the best musicians at their own game, because you'll probably look silly. Instead, get creative and play what you play best. I'll look for an opportunity to be quirky, rather than shred, or throw in the odd B.B. King blues lick. Dig deep and play something you can really own. Jam sessions are a great way to learn and grow our skills. When we play with people better than us, we always improve because we are forced to up our game!

Sometimes at jam sessions there will be one person who plays too loud or takes long boring solos and doesn't listen to the other musicians. Don't be that person! If someone begins to solo and you can't hear them, you're probably playing too loud, so bring it down.

Jam sessions can be disorganised and chaotic at times, so don't be afraid to communicate clearly with the other musicians. If you've just finished taking a solo, it's common etiquette to "nod" the next person in. Eye-to-eye communication is so important when playing, and much easier to read than subtle musical cues. The worst thing in a jam is when someone isn't alert to these cues and just starts soloing over someone else's solo!

One more tip is to let everyone know what tune you're going to play. It seems obvious, but sometimes someone will just start playing. Those who can guess the tune will join in, but those who can't will be furiously searching through their charts to see what it might be. Make it obvious, and also count in the tune really clearly. Just be kind to the other players and that kindness will reflect back on you.

Finding Your Own Style

When I first discovered Gypsy Jazz, I immediately fell in love with it. I was inspired by the playing of Django Reinhardt, Stochelo Rosenberg and Biréli Lagrène, so I immersed myself in their music. Prior to this I'd always played electric guitar, so coming to Gypsy Jazz I found some of the old-school techniques and ways of playing quite challenging. I fell back on my electric guitar technique, but transferred it onto a Gypsy-style acoustic. As a result, almost by accident, I found my own style. My influences come from jazz, blues, pop and even rock, and all of these have found their way into the melting pot of my style. I didn't do it consciously at the time but looking back I can see how those influences contribute to the way I play.

At first, I wanted to sound like Stochelo Rosenberg before I found my own identity, and my advice to you is to consciously think about your style. Don't try to be a clone of someone else. Rather, allow your unique mix of influences to infuse your Gypsy Jazz playing, so that when you play, you are recognisably *you!* If you've always loved the blues or straight-ahead bebop, don't throw that away – allow those influences to come through in your Gypsy Jazz playing. Don't get hung up on the fact that you don't sound like Biréli or anyone else. Find your voice and play to your strengths. It's really important to *be yourself.* Think about how powerful those two words are!

I've coached many guitarists through my Gypsy Jazz Club online and always encourage them to bring their own music and sound to their playing. One student is Diego from Argentina. He's learning Gypsy Jazz, but is passionate about tango music. Recently, he played us a version of *Nuages* at a club Zoom hangout, which incorporated some fiery tango chord rolls and we all loved it. Ask yourself, *what music can I play already?* Allow your influences to shine through and form part of your Gypsy Jazz style.

Writing Your Own Music

Playing music is a creative process and an important part of this can be writing your own tunes. I've written original tunes from the very beginning of my involvement with this music, and I've been honoured that some of them have been recorded by other Gypsy Jazz guitar players that I admire. Getting creative and expressing your own ideas is part of your musical journey, so don't be afraid to get them out there. Django wrote dozens of beautiful swinging tunes and today we're all still playing them.

Writing a tune and dedicating it to a friend or loved one is a gift they will always have and remember. If you're writing something, who is the song for? With that person in mind, what mood do you want to create? Happy and upbeat? Go for a major key. Moody and passionate? Go for a minor key. Some of the tunes I've rewritten are based on chord sequences that have been around before and work. You don't need to reinvent the wheel.

If you don't know where to begin, look at what you're best at. What chord sequences do you love to play over? Take those changes and try to write a new melody over them. Hundreds of great jazz standards were written over familiar changes as players took a song form they liked and wrote a new melody.

If you'd like to get into writing more seriously, check out my course Tune Writing Secrets online masterclass. In this course I challenged myself to write five new tunes, live on camera! This is a great way to discover how much fun writing your own music can be. You can do it!

https://l.robinnolan.com/sdswy

The Gypsy Jazz Repertoire

The Gypsy Jazz repertoire is wide and varied, so there are loads of tunes that you *could* choose to learn, but it's best to begin with the absolute essentials. In Chapter Three I mentioned the five tunes you absolutely *must* know, but I'll leave you with a longer list to explore. This is a mix of Django tunes and jazz standards which have been firmly adopted into the Gypsy Jazz repertoire. Check out as many versions of these tunes as you can on Spotify or YouTube and build a playlist of your favourites.

- *Minor Swing*
- *All of Me*
- *Coquette*
- *Dark Eyes*
- *I Can't Give You Anything But Love*
- *Manoir de Mes Rêves*
- *Daphne*
- *Minor Blues*
- *J'Attendrai*
- *Swing 42*
- *Douce Ambiance*
- *Nuages*
- *I'll See You in my Dreams*
- *Lady be Good*
- *Joseph Joseph*
- *Sweet Georgia Brown*
- *Honeysuckle Rose*
- *Je Suis Seul ce Soir*
- *Djangology*
- *Bossa Dorado*
- *Troublant Bolero*
- *It Had to be You*
- *What is This Thing Called Love?*
- *Swing 39*

Conclusion

We've been on a journey through the fundamental techniques and skills needed to play Gypsy Jazz guitar. Above all, we've learnt to *keep it simple* and that we can do a lot with very little.

It wasn't by accident that we started with the rhythm guitar, as it's the rhythm that defines this music we love. Without the distinct rhythm, it ceases to be authentic Gypsy Jazz. As you progress on your musical journey, continue to develop your rhythm and accompaniment skills. This will make you a musician that other people want to play with. Don't overcomplicate things and keep it simple and groovy.

We've looked at soloing and explored how to combine licks, scales and arpeggios to create solos. Remember that you'll only need to solo over three basic chord types: major, minor and dominant. When it comes to soloing, remember to *be yourself*. Don't try to imitate anyone else.

In Pillar 3 we worked on intros and endings to help us craft arrangements and also looked at the essential skill of memorising tunes. Remember, it's better to know three songs off by heart than *kind of know* thirty. Get good at fewer songs!

In Pillar 4 we discussed the art of making music with other musicians. Skills like working with a bass player and the art of dynamics are essential skills that are easily overlooked.

We've covered a lot of ground, but keep returning to the mantras mentioned at the beginning of this book. Keep them in mind and you'll get lots of joy out of learning this music. Here's a recap!

Keep It Simple. This goes for the rhythm and soloing. Always ask yourself, *can I simplify this?*

Be Yourself. You are the best at playing like you. Don't feel pressured to sound like anyone else.

Have Fun. Make sure you have fun at all times! You don't need to suffer in the practice room.

Stay Inspired! This is my motto. Always seek inspiration, because the things that inspire you always magically improve your playing!

Robin.

Continue Your Gypsy Jazz Journey With Robin Nolan

Join The Gypsy Jazz Club

The #1 online community for learning Gypsy Jazz guitar. This is where I can personally help you achieve your guitar playing goals, week after week.

https://l.robinnolan.com/n8sgy

Gypsy Jazz Jumpstart

Go in depth to master the classic Gypsy Jazz tune *Minor Swing*. You'll be playing like a hotshot in time for the next jam!

https://l.robinnolan.com/nhxm8

Robin Nolan plays Polak Gypsy Guitars

https://www.polak-gypsyguitars.com

www.ingramcontent.com/pod-product-compliance
Lightning Source LLC
Chambersburg PA
CBHW081433090426
42740CB00017B/3290

9 781789 331981